NORTH KOREA TODAY

NORTH KOREA TODAY

Edited by

ROBERT A. SCALAPINO

FREDERICK A. PRAEGER, *Publisher*

New York • London

FREDERICK A. PRAEGER, PUBLISHER
64 UNIVERSITY PLACE, NEW YORK 3, N.Y., U.S.A.
49 GREAT ORMOND STREET, LONDON W. C. 1, ENGLAND

Published in the United States of America in 1963
by Frederick A. Praeger, Inc., Publisher

Published in the United Kingdom in 1963
by Frederick A. Praeger, Inc., Publisher

First published in Great Britain in 1963
as a special issue of *The China Quarterly*

Library of Congress Catalog Card Number: 63-20152

This book is Number 135 in the series of
Praeger Publications in Russian History and World Communism

Printed in the United States of America

Contents

NORTH KOREA TODAY

Politics in North Korea: Pre-Korean War Stage

By Chong-Sik Lee

If one were to believe the official histories written in North Korea during the past few years, political developments in North Korea after 1945 and even the entire history of the Korean Communist movement would seem to have been relatively simple. According to North Korean historians, the new proletariat took over the leadership of the struggle for national liberation after the bourgeois-led March First Movement of 1919 had failed. The Korean Communist Party, first organised in 1925, ceased to operate in 1928 because the sectarians in the Party leadership failed to establish a link with the surging movement of the workers and peasants. The national liberation movement recovered its vigour and direction in the 1930s only because Kim Il-song, whose strategy and tactics were the most scientific and most in accord with the principles of Marxism-Leninism, provided leadership. Kim Il-song became the " beacon " of the revolutionary movement, and the Korean People's Revolutionary Army under him fought against the Japanese " shoulder to shoulder with the Soviet Army."

If one were to accept this account as historically accurate, it would follow as a matter of course that Kim Il-song and his comrades-in-arms " returned home in triumph after crushing Japanese militarism " and " set about the work of organising a Marxist–Leninist Party of a new type, establishing a unified people's power throughout Korea." [1]

But the simple official history distorts the picture too grossly. Although it is known that there was an obscure Korean guerrilla leader by the name of Kim Il-song operating in the mountain region of southern Manchuria from the late 1930s to early 1940s, and that his units caused some annoyance to the Japanese security forces near the Manchurian-Korean border, he had not attained the leadership of any large segment of the Korean revolutionary movement. We have evidence that some of the Korean revolutionaries in China knew about Kim's activities as early as 1937, but there was no effective communication between the Korean revolutionaries in China and Manchuria.

Nor is it true that the Korean people spontaneously rallied around Kim's leadership after 1945. The political situation in North Korea at

[1] *Facts About Korea* (Pyongyang: Foreign Languages Publishing House, 1961), p. 33.

the time of the Japanese surrender was much more complicated and delicate than the Communists make it out to be. Kim Il-song was little known among the Korean people, and he could never have attained his present position without Russian help.

Amid the confusion of the North Korean political scene in 1945, we can identify four major forces: the domestic Communist group, the returnees from China who were subsequently identified as the Yenan faction, the returnees from Russia who entered Korea with the Soviet forces, and the non-Communist nationalist group. Political struggles among the first three groups have continued ever since the liberation of Korea in August 1945. The fourth group, however, was soon suppressed by the Russian occupation authorities.

Quite contrary to current Communist assertions, the political group that had the most vitality and potentiality in North Korea was the last named. Indeed, the Japanese governor in Pyongan Namdo (the province that includes Pyongyang), who had the best available information on the distribution of power among Korean political figures, transferred his authority to one of the nationalist leaders, Cho Man-sik. Even the Soviet Army which moved into North Korea, and which had established its authority over the entire area by September, found it expedient to appoint Cho as the chief of the Provisional Political Committee and later the Five Provinces Administration Bureau, a native governing body over the entire Soviet zone of occupation.

Cho Man-sik, a Christian teacher,[2] derived his power from the organised strength of the Christians. It must be realised that the religious groups were the only non-Japanese sponsored organisation of any significance tolerated by the Japanese government. Christian influence was particularly strong in North Korea because of the intensive missionary activities there since the late nineteenth century. The Japanese persecution of Korean Christians, particularly in connection with their refusal to worship at Shinto shrines, had heightened the political consciousness of the Christians far above that of the average North Korean. The Christian leaders in various provinces allied with other prominent nationalist and community leaders and formally launched the Korean Democratic Party (*Choson Minjudang*) in November 1945. Although the events of the ensuing months prevented the realisation of it, the Party had the potentiality of becoming a major political force.

[2] Cho had been a teacher, and later principal, at the famed Osan School established by An Ch'ang-ho. In 1916 he became the chairman of the board of directors of the Pyongyang Y.M.C.A. After 1927 he was principal of Sungin Middle School in Pyongyang, a Christian mission school, and later the President of Choson Ilbo, a nationalistic daily newspaper. Cho served a prison sentence for his activities during the March First Movement (1919).

But Cho Man-sik inevitably clashed with the Russian authorities. Cho reportedly opposed the Russian grain purchase and land reform programmes in North Korea, and incurred the displeasure of the Soviet command. He was adamant in opposing the decision of the foreign ministers' conference in Moscow (December 1945) to place Korea under the trusteeship of the United Nations for five years. Not being able to get Cho to change his views, and realising the effect his defiance would have if he were outside the government, the Soviet command interned him in January 1946. Cho's arrest fore-warned the non-Communist nationalist leaders that their future in North Korea was problematic, and they immediately began to flee to the South. By April, the Party's central headquarters had been moved to Seoul. The Communists, however, maintained the skeleton of the Party in North Korea by placing as its head Ch'oe Yong-gon, Kim Il-song's protégé who along with another Communist Kim Ch'aek, had occupied an important post in the Party. This version of the Party was then used to help maintain the façade of " New Democracy " in North Korea.[3]

A similar fate awaited the Ch'ondogyo Ch'ong-u-dang, the Youth Fraternal Party made up of Ch'ondogyo members. The Ch'ondogyo group, successors of the famous Tonghaks of the 1890s, had been active among the farmers since the 1930s, not only in the religious sphere but also in social and economic fields. The Youth Fraternal Party formally emerged in February 1946 as a political group and attained some strength among the farmers even after the eclipse of the Christians. But this group soon lost its independence and became merely an echo of the ruling Communists.

Another group with high hopes was the domestic Communist faction, which had been striving to build up a viable political force since the 1920s, but had suffered from internal divisions and as a result, of Japanese police suppression. For them the liberation and the Russian occupation of North Korea were a golden opportunity. They were now able to organise a movement without fear of suppression. They could not fail to build a strong force under the aegis of the Russian Army. Pak Hon-yong, a veteran Communist since the 1920s and one of the founders of the Korean Communist Party in 1925, promptly established a new headquarters in Seoul and proceeded to organise local branches throughout Korea. Although the indoctrinated Communist core was very minute, the Party encountered little difficulty in multiplying its membership. Active in North Korea were such veteran Communists as

[3] The first party conference of the Democratic Party, held in February 1946, " exposed the anti-people's policy [of Cho Man-sik and his group], expelled the traitors, and organised a new central committee around the partisan fighter, Ch'oe Yong-gon." Kim Chong-myong [Kin Sho Mei], *Chosen Shinminshushugi kakumeishi* (*History of New Democratic Revolution in Korea*) (Tokyo: Gogatsu Shobo, 1953), p. 183.

O Ki-sop, Chong Tal-hyon, Yi Chu-ha, Chu Nyong-ha, Kim Yong-bom, Pak Chong-ae, Chang Shi-u, Yi Chu-yon and Hyon Chun-hyok.

Hyon Chun-hyok was prominent not only within Communist circles but also in the overall political arena.[4] Operating in Pyongyang, he collaborated with the right-wing nationalists after the liberation and occupied the post of vice-chairman of the Provisional Political Committee. Hyon apparently reasoned that Korea was still undergoing a bourgeois revolution and that the hegemony of the revolution at that stage must be taken by the bourgeois-oriented nationalist leaders. Hyon's reasoning led to his full support of Cho Man-sik as the national symbol and supreme leader.

Evidently, however, Hyon's strategies and prominence did not please the Russian occupation authorities. Later developments clearly indicated that they did not intend to wait for a period of bourgeois revolution in North Korea. A Communist régime, albeit under the façade of " New Democracy," was to be installed as soon as possible. Obviously Hyon was not suitable for a leading role in this. Hyon was identified too closely with his own strategy and he was, perhaps, too intimately allied with the nationalists. His programme obscured the importance of communism. On September 28, 1945, he was assassinated in broad daylight on his way back from a conference with the Soviet commandant and other Communist leaders.[5] Although Hyon was given an elaborate funeral, his assassin was not apprehended. Regardless of the identity of the assassins, the murder of Hyon came at a convenient time for the other Communist factions.

Kim Il-song and his followers are reported to have arrived in North Korea early in September 1945, along with the Russian troops. They evidently spent a month analysing the political situation and making plans. On October 3, Kim was introduced by Cho Man-sik to the public as a nationalist hero[6] at a citizens' rally in Pyongyang. On October 10, the " Conference of the North Korean Five Provinces Party Representatives and Enthusiasts " were summoned in Pyongyang to organise the " North Korean Central Bureau of the Korean Communist Party," which, according to a North Korean source, was the first Korean Communist

[4] I have not been able to find any Japanese records dealing with Hyon's pre-liberation activities. But recent Japanese and Korean sources (see note 5) have him as a graduate of Keijo Imperial University who was arrested four times because of his Communist activities.

[5] Kim Ch'ang-sun, *Pukhan Sip-o-nyon-sa* (*Fifteen Years of North Korean History*) (Seoul: Chimungak, 1961), pp. 65–68; Tsuboe Senji, *Hokusen no Kaiho Junen* (*Ten Years of Liberated North Korea*) (Tokyo: Nikkan Rodo Tsushinsha, 1956), pp. 36–39.

[6] U.S. Department of State, *North Korea: A Case Study in the Techniques of Takeover*, Department of State Publication 7118 (Washington, 1961), p. 13.

Party organisation established on the principle of Marxism-Leninism and guided by true Communists.[7]

The establishment of the Central Bureau, which elected Kim Il-song first secretary, was the first step towards Kim's consolidation of power. By establishing a central organisation with the authority to control all local and provincial branches, and then by usurping power in the central headquarters, Kim was able to emasculate the opposition with relative ease. But, according to Kim's later account, resistance among the domestic faction was strong. Evidently the domestic Communists were aware of Kim's schemes and tried to avoid or delay the inevitable. In a speech delivered at the second plenum of the North Korean Workers' Party (March 1948), Kim vehemently attacked his opponents of previous days for adhering to individual heroism, sectarianism, local separatism and a multitude of other sins:

> Our Party recognised that in order to carry out the proper political duties the scattered and organisationally weak local and provincial organisations must be united under a strong central organisation in North Korea. Hence it was decided in the middle of October 1945, that the North Korean Central Committee of the Korean Communist Party be established. . . . But some of the comrades in the Party were captivated by the sectarianism of the past. They were living, just as in the past, the life of egocentricity and self-importance, confined within their small local groups, without carrying out any Party work or obeying superior organisations. Therefore, leaders of these small groups, whose vision was adjusted to their caves and who were addicted to individual heroism, opposed the establishment of the North Korean Central Bureau on the excuse that they "support the central headquarters (in Seoul)." In order to hide their schemes, [they] alleged that "establishment of the North Korean branch would result in dividing the Party."[8]

The resistance of the domestic faction was in vain. The Soviet faction under Kim was evidently beginning to be assured of its position by the middle of December, when the third enlarged conference of the

[7] Democratic People's Republic of Korea, Academy of Science, Center for Historical Studies, *Choson T'ongsa* (*Outline History of Korea*) (Hak-u Sobang reprint edition, Tokyo, 1959), III, pp. 16–17. For some reason this source and other recent publications refer to the Bureau as the Organisation Committee although Kim's "Selected Works" (*Kin Nichisei Senshu* [Kyoto: 1952], Supp. Vol., p. 43) cites it as the Central Bureau. This Japanese edition of Kim's selected works was edited by Korean Communists in Japan.

[8] *Ibid.* A later publication further specified the charges implicating Pak Hon-yong as the leader of Kim's opposition. "But the Pak Hon-yong group, realising the fatal consequence to themselves of establishing the North Korean Organisation Committee, opposed its organisation to the utmost." Han Im-hyok, *Kim Il-song Tongji e Uihan Choson Kongsandang Ch'anggon* (*Establishment of the Korean Communist Party by Comrade Kim Il-song*) (Pyongyang: Korean Workers' Party Press, 1961), p. 32. Alleged agents and followers of Pak in North Korea were O Ki-sop, Chu Nyong-ha, Yi Chu-ha, Chang Shi-u and Chang Sun-myong. *Ibid.* p. 26.

executive Committee of the North Korean Central Bureau was held in Pyongyang.[9] Kim's followers, both Soviet Koreans (Koreans born and raised in Russia) and Russian-trained Koreans, had been busy infiltrating the central, provincial and local Communist establishments in North Korea. Also, to consolidate his newly-gained position, Kim ordered a sweeping purge:

> The third enlarged committee . . . decided to wage a struggle against all reactionary elements infiltrated into the Party. In order to guarantee ideological unity and organisational harmony, the Party re-examined the members, issued membership certificates, expelled pro-Japanese and reactionary elements, and struck a great blow against those who violated the political policies of the central headquarters, those local separatists who had liberalistic and sectarian inclinations . . ., and those who adhered to leftist opportunism against the political course of the central headquarters.[10]

No doubt the Party needed purging. In their haste to mobilise new comrades in the excitement of their new freedom, local Party organisations had enlisted persons of unknown quality fairly indiscriminately. A considerable proportion of these were, no doubt, opportunists. Many deserters and renegades from the Party during the preceding period had also returned to the ranks. If the Party was to acquire any sense of order and discipline, some tightening-up was essential. If the purge was a necessity, however, it was also a convenient tool for those in power. Such general charges as sectarianism and individual heroism are universally applicable to any Communist, regardless of nationality. The Korean Communist movement has been particularly notorious for its factional strife. In this sense, the fact that Kim himself had not been involved in the pre-liberation Communist movement within Korea was a distinct advantage. It is impossible, however, to exclude him from the charges of individual heroism and sectarianism.

While Kim Il-song was consolidating his power under the aegis of the Soviet authorities, the Yenan group was also actively engaged in establishing itself in the North Korean political arena. The Yenan group had some prominent figures among its leaders. Kim Tu-bong, at least twenty years senior to Kim Il-song, was an established literary scholar before his self-imposed exile to China in 1919. Although he had associated with left-wing nationalists and Communists in China (*e.g.*, Kim Rip, Yi Tong-hwi) as early as 1919, he had also associated with right-wing nationalists (*e.g.*, Kim Ku). Having been the head of the Korean Independence League *(Choson Tongnip Tongmaeng)*

[9] "By the time of the third enlarged conference, the Korean Communist Party's organisation, from the central guiding organ down to the cells, was firmly established, and the Party organisation began to develop into a disciplined combatant fortress closely aligned with the masses." *Choson T'ongsa*, III, p. 20.

[10] *Kin Nichisei Senshu*, I, p. 268.

in Yenan (organised in 1942) and having had the experience of working closely with the Chinese Communist leaders, Kim was an obvious asset to the North Korean Communists. Ch'oe Ch'ang-ik, an active left-wing intellectual even before his exile to China, was also well known.[11]

Another asset the Yenan faction possessed was its trained military personnel. Most of Kim Il-song's immediate followers claimed partisan and hence military background, and Kim Il-song himself reportedly wore a Russian major's uniform when he arrived in Korea, but the Yenan faction possessed the larger number of trained and disciplined troops. The Korean Volunteers' Corps (later Army), established under the guidance of the Chinese Nationalist government and later developed under the aegis of the Chinese Communists, had at least three to four hundred veteran officers at the time of the Japanese surrender. Since then it had multiplied its forces by enlisting a large number of young Koreans in North China and Manchuria.[12]

The Yenan group entered North Korean politics with its old designation, the Independence League. Since the various other Communist Party factions had pre-empted the poorest elements of the population, particularly in the Hamgyong provinces where O Ki-sop was one of the leaders, the League focused attention on winning the office workers, the petty bourgeoisie, and the intelligentsia. According to Kim Ch'ang-sun, a former communist journalist in North Korea, many Korean bureaucrats in Japanese government service joined the Yenan group as a " political security " measure.[13] As a result the Independence League—redesignated the New People's Party (*Shinmindang*) in March 1946—consisted mainly of literate and well-to-do elements, whereas the Communist Party had a preponderance of the illiterate and indigent.

In spite, or perhaps because of these differences, the leaders of the two groups maintained close co-operation, at least in their outward manifestations. For example, when the North Korean Provisional People's Committee was established in Pyongyang in February 1946, as a precursor of the régime to be established later, the two factions shared the leading positions. Kim Il-song occupied the chairmanship and Kim Tu-bong the vice-chairmanship. The second vice-chairmanship went to a member of the Korean Democratic Party.

11 I dealt with the Yenan group in detail in Chaps. xi–xii of my forthcoming book, *The Politics of Korean Nationalism* (Berkeley & Los Angeles: Un. of California Press, 1963).

12 These officers and troops were soon integrated into the North Korean police and security forces and eventually became the core of the " Korean People's Army." For details see Roy E. Appleman, *The United States Army in the Korean War: South to the Naktong, North to the Yalu (June–November 1950)* (Washington: Office of the Chief of Military History, Department of the Army, 1961), pp. 8–9.

13 Kim Ch'ang-sun, *op. cit.*, p 98.

Detailed facts regarding the negotiations between the two dominant groups in North Korea are not known, but their leaders seem to have come to an agreement that the separate existence of two rival Communist groups would be harmful to the total cause:

> At this kind of historical stage, the power of our working masses must not be splintered. . . . In order to accomplish the great democratic tasks laid before the Korean people, a united power of the working masses—a strong vanguard party—is necessary.[14]

Because of this necessity, according to Kim Il-song, the leaders of the New People's Party proposed the merger of the two Parties, to which the Communist Party leadership agreed with enthusiasm. Soon officials of both Parties at various levels began to have joint conferences regarding the merger, and the entire membership approved the plan.[15] The inaugural conference of the North Korean Workers' Party was held at the end of July 1946.

An interesting aspect of the three-day conference was the choice of the leadership. In view of the fact that Kim Il-song already occupied the foremost position in the government mechanism in North Korea and Kim Tu-bong was the second man in line, it would have been logical to expect the same order to be maintained in the amalgamated Party. But in the new Party the order was reversed, with Kim Tu-bong at the helm. Kim Il-song was relegated to the vice-chairmanship along with a relatively insignificant leader of the domestic faction, Chu Nyong-ha. We have no access to the official record of the conference and the more recent documents do not explain this rather odd turn of events. But one of the delegates present at the conference, Kim Ch'ang-sun, offers an interesting explanation, illuminating the subtle relationship existing between the Soviet and Yenan factions.

According to Kim Ch'ang-sun, the Communist Party was indeed planning to make Kim Il-song chairman. The first speaker at the session on membership of the central committee declared: "It is a determined fact (or matter of course) that our sagacious national leader Kim Il-song should be elected the chairman of the North Korean Workers' Party." But this matter-of-fact announcement and the excessive eulogy of Kim Il-song by this speaker made the delegates of the Yenan faction restless and uneasy. Their unfavourable reaction was so obvious that the Russian colonel present on the dais as an honoured guest advised a temporary recess. Upon reconvening, a Communist delegate, O Ki-sop, argued (as instructed) that the chairman need not necessarily be Kim Il-song, and his speech won thunderous applause

[14] *Kin Nichisei Senshu*, I, pp. 81–82.

[15] *Ibid.* p. 82. The total membership at this time was 366,000, of which 73,000 were of worker origin and 105,000 of poor peasant origin. *Ibid.* Supp. Vol., pp. 47–48.

from the New People's Party delegates. Peace in the Party being restored, at the Central Executive Committee meeting, Kim Il-song nominated Kim Tu-Bong to be the first chairman of the North Korean Workers' Party. Underlying this event, according to Kim Ch'ang-sun, was the feeling of insecurity on the part of the Yenan group. Many delegates of the New People's Party were uncertain of the meaning of the merger and secretly suspected that the call for unity was only a manoeuvre to allow Kim Il-song to absorb the New People's Party's forces. In order to allay this fear, Kim Il-song had to yield the chairmanship to Kim Tu-bong.[16]

It would be naïve, of course, to believe that the election of Kim Tu-bong to the chairmanship actually altered the power relationship We must keep in mind that North Korea was under Russian occupation until the end of 1948. Regardless of the actual strength of the Yenan group, Kim Il-song was still the vital link between the North Korean Communists and the Soviet military command, and no one could effectively challenge Kim Il-song's power. In spite of early expectations and aspirations, the Chinese Communists took very little, if any, part in North Korean politics.[17]

As on the occasion of the establishment of the North Korean Central Bureau of the Communist Party, there were some among the Party leadership who disliked the merger. Some of the Communists held a " self-righteous and haughty attitude " towards the New People's Party and objected to the merger on the ground that the Communist Party would become petty bourgeois in outlook.[18] Since the New People's Party was known to be milder on the issues of treatment of the middle classes, land reform and religion than were the doctrinaire Communists,[19] the charges of the opposition were justifiable ones. By agreeing to the proposal for a merger (or proposing it) the Party leadership was committing a serious theoretical error, particularly if Kim Il-song were willing to apply the standard pronounced by himself.

At the inaugural conference of the Workers' Party, Kim had asserted that

16 Kim Ch'ang-sun, *op. cit.*, pp. 99–101. Kim Il-song reported: " There have been attempts to falsify the recent merger as a scheme of the Communists, and the reactionary elements are spreading this kind of false rumour." *Kin Nichisei Senshu*, I, p. 105.

17 See U.S. Department of State, *op. cit.*, p. 115, and Chong-Sik Lee, " Korean Communists and Yenan," *The China Quarterly*, No. 9, January–March 1962, pp. 182–192.

18 *Kin Nichisei Senshu*, I, pp. 82–83.

19 U.S. Department of State, *op. cit.*, p. 115. Kim Il-song stated in his report at the Pyongan Namdo Party enthusiasts' conference (Sept. 9, 1946) that some individuals rejected Marxism-Leninism as the guiding doctrine of the Workers' Party. Some others said that the Communists must abandon Marxism-Leninism when the Workers' Party was established. *Kin Nichisei Senshu*, I, p. 103.

> . . . the Workers' Party is a combat unit and the vanguard of the working masses. We must fight with our utmost to maintain the Party's purity, unity, and iron discipline. If we were to fight against the enemy without meeting these conditions within our ranks, it would be nothing less than folly.[20]

Here Kim Il-song was obviously referring to the Leninist principle of a Communist Party being the vanguard of the proletariat. But both the Communist and the New People's Parties were deficient in the requisite qualities. A majority of the members of both Parties lacked ideological education and training. Indeed, Kim complained of the paucity of ideological education among the Party members many years later. It would have been a major task to raise the standards of Communist Party members to what might be considered the norm, even without a merger with another, more heterogeneous, group. It would have been necessary to execute a major purge at this juncture in order to improve the quality of the Party membership. Kim objected to this proposal, however, by saying that it was just nothing but a "passive expression of opposition to the Party merger." It was practically impossible to foresee the Party Kim seems to have envisaged. "Popularisation" of the proletarian party and the notion of a disciplined vanguard were obviously poles apart. Kim Il-song, the self-appointed theoretician of the North Korean Communist Party, however, dismissed these charges and contradictions merely as fabrications of left-wing deviationists and sectarians who "not only did not understand the policies of our Party but also the simple truth that revolution can be attained only through the consolidation of all revolutionary comrades and the unity of the entire masses."[21] It is interesting to note that most of the sectarian left-wing deviationists belonged to the domestic-faction Communists.

Although theoretical contradictions were obvious in Kim Il-song's pronouncements and policies, the merger of the two Parties into the Workers' Party was sound political tactics. This fact stands out particularly if we take the events of the next several years into consideration. As Kim Tu-bong pointed out at the inaugural conference of the Workers' Party, the Communist Party was lopsided, having many peasant and worker members but lacking intellectuals; the situation in the New People's Party was exactly the reverse.[22] By merging all of them into one political party "a strong unity" of these classes was made possible. The crucial question, of course, was for whom the stronger

[20] *Ibid.* p. 83.
[21] *Ibid.*
[22] Quoted in Kim Chong-myong, *op. cit.*, p. 188. Kim Il-song also referred to the Communist Party as that of the proletariat and the New People's Party as the representatives of farmers and intelligentsia. *Kin Nichisei Senshu*, I, p. 269.

unity was more advantageous. It has since become clear that the leaders of the Yenan faction in effect delivered their organised strength to Kim Il-song in 1946 and gradually faded from the scene, their usefulness being exhausted. Among the leaders of the Yenan group purged during and after the Korean War were Kim Tu-bong, Ch'oe Ch'ang-ik, Mu Chong and Yun Kong-hum.[23]

The immediate gains for Kim Il-song were no less significant. By absorbing the more literate and educated elements in North Korea, the Communist camp as a whole acquired a degree of respectability. The new Party was no longer a party of the poor and ignorant. Having intelligentsia, petty bourgeoisie, and office workers in the Party was particularly important because these elements were rapidly becoming leaders of opinion in their communities. The wealthier and better educated bourgeois elements, who had directed public opinion in the past, were rapidly losing their voice in public affairs—often as a result of intimidation—and the role of the New People's Party intelligentsia became ever more important.

Kim Il-song could also have foreseen the advantage of thrusting the leaders of the Yenan group into the political battles within the Communist Party. Some of the domestic Communists had large followings in different localities and their power and status were not easily assailable. Although naked power was available to the Russian faction, thanks to the support provided by the Soviet command, repeated use of violence against prominent Communists was not altogether desirable. Merging the Yenan group with the Communist Party was a less conspicuous way of defeating domestic-faction rivals.

The events of the succeeding years attest to the above hypothesis. A major purpose of the second plenum of the North Korean Workers' Party, in 1948, was to dismantle the domestic faction. Such leaders as O Ki-sop, Chong Tal-hyon, Ch'oe Yong-dal and Yi Pong-su were attacked for sectarianism, local separatism and individual-heroism.[24] Although O Ki-sop, a former vice-chairman of the North Korean Communist Party, was still included in the sixty-seven-member Central Committee, he was relegated to a minor post in a government-operated enterprise. A reported large-scale purge of the rank and file in early 1947, which is said to have affected between 40,000 to 60,000 persons,[25] may have had a direct connection with developments at the second plenum.

[23] For details see Ilpyong Y. Kim's contribution (p. 94).

[24] Kim Ch'ang-sun, *op. cit.*, p. 105. Kim Il-song's speech at the March 1948 plenum has already been cited. (See note 8.)

[25] U.S. Department of State, *op. cit.*, p. 14. According to Kim Il-song, the strength of the party rose from 366,000 in July 1946, to more than 700,000 in January 1948. *Kin Nichisei Senshu*, Supp. Vol., pp. 47–48.

The final act of the pre-war political drama in North Korea was enacted in June 1949, when the North Korean Communists absorbed the South Korean Workers' Party. Undoubtedly the merger of these two organisations into the Korean Workers' Party signified the ultimate triumph of Kim Il-song. For the merger in effect signified the conclusion of a long-drawn out contest between Kim and Pak Hon-yong, obviously in Kim's favour.

In spite of all the invectives used by present-day Communist historians against Pak (*e.g.*, " agent, spy and running-dog of American imperialism "), he was truly the elder statesman of the Korean Communist movement. Pak had been active as a young Communist as early as 1921, when he had served as secretary of the Korean Communist Youth League (or Komsomol) in Shanghai,[26] and he was one of the first Korean Communists to be held in Japanese prisons. He was also one of the first to raise the red flag in Korea after the Japanese defeat. Unlike Kim Il-song, furthermore, Pak's name and his past record were common knowledge throughout Korea.

By 1949, however, Pak's status was far inferior to that of Kim Il-song, who by this time was the premier of the Democratic People's Republic (established in September 1948) and the undisputed leader of the party. In November 1946, under pressure from the North Korean Communists, Pak and others amalgamated parts of the Korean Communist Party (of South Korea), the People's Party (the *Inmingdang* of Yo Un-hyong), and the New People's Party (of South Korea, led by Ho Hon)[27] into the South Korean Workers' Party. Although the leftist camp in South Korea split into two groups, the other being the Working People's Party (*Kullo Inmindang*, under Yo), Pak's organisation at one point attained the support of 370,000 members.[28] Pak's South Korean Workers' Party, however, was vexed with the same problems that afflicted the Communist movement of the pre-liberation era, namely factional divisions and government suppression. Although the Communist movement was officially outlawed in South Korea only

26 Robert A. Scalapino and Chong-Sik Lee, " The Origins of the Korean Communist Movement (I)," *Journal of Asian Studies*, XX, No. 1 (November 1960), 19, pp. 162–163.

27 Yo Un-hyong (sometimes spelled Lyuh Woon Hyung) was a progressive nationalist of renown. Ho Hon, a lawyer, defended the Korean Communists in Japanese courts. Yo was assassinated in Seoul in 1947. Ho went to North Korea and became the first president of the Supreme People's Congress.

28 Yi Ki-ha, *Hanguk chongdang paltalsa* (*History of the Development of Korean Political Parties*) (Seoul: Uihoe chongch'isa, 1961), pp. 138–147. Although this is an uneven book, it presents a useful outline of the political events in South Korea. Kim Ch'ang-sun (*op. cit.*, p. 119) agrees with Yi's estimate. Kim Il-song did not mention the size of the South Korean Party, but did state in 1956 that " the Pak group carried out fivefold and tenfold movements to show that the South Korean Party was numerically superior to the North Korean Party." *Kim Il-song Sonjip* (*Selected Works of Kim Il-song*) (Pyongyang: Korean Workers' Party Press, 1960), IV, p. 534.

on December 1, 1948, the Communists had to go underground long before this date. As a result, the movement was gradually paralysed and in early 1948 Pak and his top-level comrades abandoned their home ground for North Korea.

Pak was forced to abandon the attitude of superiority he had once maintained towards Kim. As suggested earlier, Pak evidently opposed the establishment of the North Korean Central Bureau of the Communist Party in 1946 for fear that this would endanger his central leadership. According to Kim Il-song's later account, Pak also objected to the proposal advanced at a joint conference of the leaders of the southern and northern Parties (held around 1946) for an all-nation Party conference that might elect a central committee and adopt Party platforms and rules.[29] Since Pak's organisation in Seoul was already regarded by Pak and his followers throughout Korea as the "central headquarters," Pak probably did not see the need for the proposed conference. But once the central headquarters in Seoul had disintegrated and its officers had moved to Pyongyang, Pak could no longer refute the argument that the two workers' Parties must be united in order "to strengthen Party activities in South Korea and to guarantee the unified guidance of the two workers' Parties." Pak had already accepted the posts of vice-premier and foreign minister in the Kim régime. Pak may have decided that it would be more expedient to merge the two entities and consolidate his power by acquiring allies within the new organisation.[30] Or he may have thought that the consolidated power of the North Korean régime and the united Party could be used to regain the lost ground in South Korea.[31] At any rate, it was impossible for Pak to challenge Kim effectively. Kim Il-song was installed as chairman of the united Korean Workers' Party, the supreme leader of the Communist movement in Korea, and Pak had to be content with the Vice-chairmanship which he shared with a Soviet-faction man, Ho Ka-i. Kim Tu-bong, the former chairman of the North Korean Workers' Party, still retained his posts in the Central Committee, but was deprived of his more

29 *Ibid.* p. 532.

30 According to the North Korean Premier, Pak and his followers spread poisonous germs in the hitherto healthy North Korean Party and collected around their coterie such enemies of the people as Ho Ka-i (a former Russian citizen and vice-chairman of the Workers' Party), Chu Nyong-ha (former vice-chairman of the North Korean Workers' Party, domestic faction), Pak Il-u (a leader of the Yenan faction, one time Minister of Home Affairs), and other sectarians still remaining in North Korea. *Ibid.* p. 536.

31 Kim Sam-gyu, a former editor of the influential *Tong-a Ilbo* (Seoul) and now an advocate of "neutral Korea," advanced the thesis that Pak's anxiety about the destruction of his forces in South Korea and his assessment of the public opinion in South Korea was largely responsible for the beginning of the Korean War. *Konnichi no Chosen* (*Korea Today*) (Tokyo: Kawade Shobo, 1956), pp. 51–103.

pretentious title; he received a consolation prize in the presidency of the presidium of the Supreme People's Congress.

Thus politics in North Korea were very slippery, and far more complicated than contemporary Communist historians make out. Of course, the simplified historiography of North Korea is not totally without merit, for the political history of North Korea is essentially a history of the rise of one man. Kim Il-song is the sole winner, the hero, the omnipotent one. Achievements and contributions made by the villains are cancelled out by their sundry crimes and sins, and presumably there is no need to digress on these individuals.

The environment in North Korea was favourable for the rise of Kim Il-song. The presence of Russian troops in North Korea until the end of 1948 and the full support given by the Soviet command were the most crucial factors in his ascent to power. And yet, one must not underrate the capabilities of the man himself. North Korean propagandists were right in asserting that Kim Il-song is a "faithful disciple of Stalin." He appears to have imitated the Soviet dictator in his thoroughly Machiavellian methods of removing his colleagues.

Kim's strategy and tactics are not unique. Violence, the merger of rival groups, propaganda and purges are familiar tools of any successful Communist. The factors that have distinguished Kim from his rivals have been his greater skill as a strategist and tactician, and his receipt of effective support at the opportune time.

The Post-War Politics of Communist Korea

By GLENN D. PAIGE AND DONG JUN LEE

> I want to say with all the strength at my command that there is no Communist country in the world where human beings are deprived of every basic freedom and driven like animals within the confines of an organisation as tight as an iron pail—all for the power and luxury of a handful of Communist rulers—as they are in Communist North Korea under the Kim Il-song puppet dictatorship.
>
> Dong Jun Lee, 1961.[1]

THE establishment of Communist power in North Korea represents one more example of the triumph of purposive political behaviour over impersonal economic and social forces [2] and as such merits the attention of all those who are concerned about the survival of the theory and practice of a free society in a shrinking world. If purposive Communist behaviour can become the prime mover of history, then so can the dedicated efforts of those with different conceptions of ends and means in the solution of human problems.

The shock troops for the accomplishment of socio-economic change in North Korea since 1945 have been the members of the Korean Workers' Party (KWP) and its antecedents. Their mission is prescribed in the first article of the 1956 party regulations: "The immediate goal of the Korean Workers' Party is to complete the anti-imperialist, anti-feudal, democratic revolution on a national scale; the final goal is the construction of a Communist society." If size is a correlate of organisational power, the KWP has been growing in ability to act upon Korean society somewhat as follows: 4,000 alleged Communists in 1945; 360,000 members claimed at the time of the First Congress in 1946; 750,000 at the Second Congress in 1948; 1,164,695 at the Third Congress in 1956; and 1,311,563 members, or about 12 per cent. of a total population estimated at 10,700,000, at the Fourth Congress in 1961. Changes in the composition of the KWP have been accompanied by changes in the characteristics of the North Korean population: as the proportion of

1 *Hwansanggwa Hyonsil: Naui Kongsanjuui Kwan* (*Fantasy and Fact: My Observations of Communism*) (Seoul: Tongbang T'ongsinsa, 1961), p. 222.

2 Robert V. Daniels, "The Chinese Revolution in Russian Perspective," *World Politics*, XIII (January 1961), p. 230.

total population classified as "urban" increased from 17·7 per cent. in 1953 to 40·6 per cent. in 1960, the proportion of KWP members classified as "workers" increased from 17·3 per cent. to 30·0 per cent. between the Third and Fourth Congresses.[3] The ability of the KWP to achieve social change has been augmented by close ties with its main allies, the Communist Parties of Russia (CPSU) and China (CPC), and by the temporary massive military presence of Russian and Chinese forces. Thus, for example, land reform was carried out during the early period of Red Army occupation, 1945–48, while the collectivisation of agriculture was completed during the encampment of the Chinese People's "Volunteers," 1950–58.

In the present article we shall concentrate upon some of the major political developments which have taken place in North Korea during the period 1953–62. After some comments upon the North Korean situation at the signing of the Armistice Agreement on July 27, 1953, we propose to centre our discussion upon three main problem areas: factional politics within the KWP; inter-party politics among the KWP, CPSU and the CPC; and the politics of Korean unification.

The Post-war Situation

The Armistice was greeted with relief and approval by the people of North Korea. The strains and privations of the war—incessant bombing, prolonged fear, extended working hours, food shortages, and loss of relatives—had resulted in widespread "war-weariness" (*yomjonjuui*, lit., hate war-ism). During the conflict, however, there had developed a striking ambivalence in attitudes toward military violence: on the one hand, it was abhorred; on the other, it was welcomed since it might bring quick victory to one of the antagonists and the end of mass killing.

The war-time experience was accompanied by the development of certain unfavourable attitudes toward the KWP and the Soviet Union as well as by the growth of certain favourable attitudes toward Communist China. The principal discontent with the KWP was that it had not been vigorous enough in its relief and reconstruction work. It was popularly regarded in this respect as the "do-nothing" party. The Soviet Union suffered in popular esteem because it had not given greater assistance to the North Korean war effort. The North Koreans were aware that South Korea was free from Communist air attack and therefore hoped for direct retaliation by Soviet airpower against American attacks upon the North. The knowledge that Russian fighter

[3] Kim Il-song, "Otchetnyi doklad Tsentral'nogo Komiteta Trudovoi Partii Korei IV s'ezdu partii," *Izbrannye Stat'i i Rechi* (Moscow: State Publishing House for Political Literature, 1962), p. 795.

pilots were flying defensively over North Korean territory and that the Russians were providing military and relief supplies did not satisfy the demand for deeper Soviet military commitment, including the participation of Soviet infantry divisions. By contrast, the North Koreans were favourably impressed by Chinese military assistance. Mao Tse-tung's injunction to the Chinese soldiers in Korea to " love the Korean Democratic People's Republic, the Korean Workers' Party, and the Korean people as your own government, party, and people—and treasure every mountain, every stream, every tree, and every blade of grass the same," [4] was widely respected and appreciated. This did not mean, however, that Korean-Chinese relations were without points of friction. There was some evidence of professional jealousy, for example, among North Korean army officers who had to take orders from Chinese commanders.

Despite the war-time destructiveness and psychological strains there were few signs of social malaise in North Korea at the end of the war. There appeared to be little murder, theft and personal violence, although there were growing signs of sexual licence, especially among the young. Thus, while there were points of popular dissatisfaction, basic KWP control over the people of North Korea was not in jeopardy. The Communist version of how the war began was still widely believed even though some people had heard the truth about the Communist initiative during the northward advance of the Republic of Korea Army in the fall of 1950. Many persons who might have formed centres of anti-Communist resistance had taken advantage of war-time chaos to escape to the South. Furthermore, the presence of the Chinese army discouraged thoughts that anti-Communist political activity could be successful.

The Armistice, however, brought the end to the war-time pressures for cohesion within the factional coalition which had been built as the KWP after 1945; intra-Party factional strife again came out into the open. Post-war developments in this respect need to be placed in pre-war perspective. The KWP might be described as having been compounded of five main factional elements: (1) the immediate associates of Kim Il-song, known as the " Kapsan " faction after the group of Communists operating in the area of the North Korean town of Kapsan who are alleged to have supported him during his Manchurian guerrilla days in the 1930s and 1940s; (2) the " Soviet-Koreans," who had returned in the van of the Red Army but had not been active

[4] Kim Il-song, " Chojung yangguk inminui chont'ujok uui " (" The Militant Friendship of the Korean and Chinese Peoples "), *Kim Il-song Sonjip* (*Selected Works of Kim Il-song*), IV (Pyongyang: KWP Press, 1960), p. 444. Hereafter this source will be cited as *Selected Works*.

as a group in the Korean independence movement prior to 1945; (3) the "Yenan-Koreans," who had been associated with the CPC before 1945; (4) the domestic North Korean Communists who had been active under Japanese rule, and (5) the domestic South Korean Communists, who had their primary social connections in the area below the Thirty-eighth Parallel and who had been active in the South Korean Workers' Party led by Pak Hon-yong until it was outlawed in 1948. In the pre-1953 period the factional balance of power had proceeded through a number of subtle shifts, all of which can be seen in retrospect as working toward the eventual advantage of the Kapsan faction. First, Kim Il-song was put in power as an obvious figurehead with real support rooted in the Soviet occupation forces and the Soviet-Koreans. In order to rule, the Kapsan faction first allied with the Soviet- and Yenan-Koreans to remove North Korean Communists such Hyon Chun-hyok, Chu Yong-ha, and Oh Ki-sop as contenders for leadership prior to 1950. This is known as the purge of the *kungnae* (domestic) faction. During the war, two figures of major importance for factional politics were eliminated: the popular Yenan-Korean general Mu Chong, by censure, imprisonment, and eventual exile to China (at Chinese request) in 1950; and the Soviet-Korean Party leader Ho Kai, by censure and suicide in 1951. We now turn to the struggles of the post-war period which incidentally reveal the vitality of Korean political traditions.

Intra-Party Politics

> Over the years, as you well know, factional disputes have taken place in many Parties. There are Parties which have achieved a certain amount of notoriety in this respect such as the American and Polish Parties, but the Korean factions hold the record.
>
> Otto Kuusinen, 1931.[5]

> In the course of our persistent struggle against the anti-Party factional elements and their evil ideological influence, the Party has been able to extirpate factionalism . . . and has completed the historic task of achieving the complete unity of the Korean Communist movement.
>
> Kim Il-song, 1961.[6]

Although the Kapsan faction appears to have gained a decisive victory over its competitors in the post-war period, the history of Korean politics and of the international Communist movement argues against the conclusion that factional conflict has disappeared as a force in

[5] Otto Kuusinen, "O koreiskom kommunisticheskom dvizhenii," *Revolyutsionnyi vostok*, Nos. 11–12 (1931), p. 108.
[6] Kim Il-song, "Otchetnyi doklad . . . ," p. 793.

North Korea. The predominance of the Kapsan faction can be illustrated by the composition of the eleven-man Standing Committee of the Central Committee of the KWP which was confirmed in power at the Fourth Congress in September 1961: Kim Il-song, Pak Kum-ch'ol, Kim Il, Kim Kwang-hyop, Ch'oe Yong-gon, Nam Il, Kim Ch'ang-man, Pak Chong-ae, Chong Il-yong, Yi Hyo-sun, and Yi Chong-ok. At least the first four of these can be clearly identified with the Kapsan faction. They are believed to be in strategic positions of control over the party (Pak Kum-ch'ol, vice-chairman of the KWP and chief of the organisational bureau), bureaucracy (Kim Il, first vice-premier), and army (Kim Kwang-hyop, vice-premier and minister of defence). Kim Il-song holds all three reins of power as Party chairman, cabinet premier, and commander-in-chief. We can identify only one leader in each case associated with the formerly potent Soviet-Korean (Nam Il) and Yenan-Korean (Kim Ch'ang-man) factions. The remaining members of the committee are popularly believed to owe their positions to the favour of Kim Il-song.

The post-war emergence of Kim Il-song and the Kapsan faction as the locus of real power in North Korea took place in two clearly defined stages.[7] In the first stage, 1953–55, the South Korean Communists led by Pak Hon-yong were eliminated as rivals. Following a special military court-martial held in Pyongyang during August 3–6, 1953, immediately after the signing of the Armistice, Pak and his followers were purged on charges that they were "American spies" who planned to overthrow the Korean Democratic People's Republic and to establish a new revolutionary government. Of twelve key defendants, the court sentenced ten to death, including Yi Sung-yop, one of three secretaries of the KWP Central Committee. It was charged that Yi had planned to carry out a *coup d'état* against the Kim Il-song leadership through the employment of some 4,000 guerrillas of South Korean origin whom he had been training for southern operations during the late stages of the war. Although it was contended that the objective of the coup was to instal Pak Hon-yong as premier, nothing was heard about him until December 1955 when it was announced that he had been executed as an "American spy." The long delay between charges and execution seems to have been a concession to the belief that Pak was extremely influential in South Korean politics as well as within the KWP. With the passage of time the charge of Pak's American involvement seemed to gain popular credence and he was put to death without anticipated discontent.

[7] The most important published account of KWP politics from 1945 to 1960 is Kim Ch'angsun, ***Pukhan Sibonyon Sa*** **(*Fifteen Year History of North Korea*)** **(Seoul:** Chimungak, 1961), p. 283 *et seq*. We have drawn freely upon this source.

It is noteworthy that the elimination of the South Korean Communist faction was accompanied by the announcement of two major policies embodied in the Three-Year Plan (1954–56) for post-war economic reconstruction: the decision to use foreign aid primarily for heavy industrial development rather than for the satisfaction of consumer needs; and the decision to proceed with the collectivisation of agriculture. The Pak group might have opposed both policies: the first, because it would not recognise popular desires for improved living conditions; the second, because it would alienate the farmers of South Korea and thus prolong Korean partition. There was no public discussion of this possibility, however.

In the second stage of post-war factional struggle, 1956–58, the Yenan-Koreans led by Kim Tu-bong and Ch'oe Ch'ang-ik, were swept from positions of authority. The precipitant occasion was the August Plenum of the Central Committee of the KWP which followed the Third Congress in April 1956. Among the public charges later hurled at the Yenan-Koreans was that they " dogmatically wanted to follow the experience of other countries." [8] During the August Plenum, the Yenan-Koreans, spearheaded by Yun Kong-hum, had taken the offensive against the " personality cult of Kim Il-song " and his " dictatorial style of leadership " in the same spirit as the attack upon Stalin at the Twentieth Congress of the CPSU. Among other Yenan-Korean demands were that the KWP relinquish control over the Supreme People's Assembly (Kim Tu-bong), that the trade unions be freed from subservience to the Party (So Hwi), and that the distorted history of the Korean Communist movement which portrays the Kapsan faction as the " only true Communists " be rectified (Ch'oe Ch'ang-ik). After a plenum struggle, the Yenan-Koreans and their anti-Kim allies were vanquished. Yun Kong-hum and at least four other prominent leaders escaped to China in fear of their lives. All those suspected of sympathy with the anti-Kim attack were expelled from the KWP and governmental positions. The most prestigious leader of the Yenan-Koreans, Kim Tu-bong, who had preceded Kim Il-song as the first chairman of the KWP and later served as chairman of the Standing Committee of the Supreme People's Assembly, was ousted from the Party and the latter position although his name was not formally withdrawn until the Assembly elections of 1957. By early 1958 the Yenan-Koreans had been eliminated as an intra-Party force.

[8] Kim Il-song, *Modun munje haegyoreso chungsim korirul t'unt'unhi turo chapko kue yogyangul chipchung haja* (*In Solving all Problems Let us Grasp the Central Link and Concentrate all our Forces There*) (Pyongyang: KWP Press, 1959), p. 12.

The ouster of the Yenan-Koreans was also accompanied by the reaffirmation of the Third Congress decision to continue the emphasis upon heavy industry in the execution of the first Five-Year Plan (1957–61). The Yenan-Koreans and other members of the August opposition had opposed this policy. In October 1959, Kim Il-song condemned them, saying, "If we had followed their views, we would not have reached today's level of industrial development in fifty years." [9] It is important to note that in declaring 1960 as the Year of Shock Absorption, in easing heavy industrial expansion in the first four years of the Seven-Year Plan (1961–67), and in stressing food, clothing and housing among the Six Peaks to be scaled in 1962, the Kapsan faction seems at last to have adopted some of the economic policies advocated by its Yenan-Korean and perhaps South Korean critics.

During the post-war years the position of the Soviet Koreans, or "SKs" in Russian as they are known in Pyongyang, seems to have suffered a subtle form of erosion. Pak Ch'ang-ok, vice premier and successor to Ho Kai as leader of the Soviet-Koreans, was ousted from the KWP in the aftermath of the August Plenum. He had written a letter to Premier Khrushchev after the Third Congress to complain that Kim Il-song was not complying with the Twentieth Congress decisions about the style of party leadership. In general, the "SKs" were not popular in North Korea; they seemed to have an arrogant air of cultural superiority. Their special privileges, such as the right to purchase goods in stores reserved for Soviet citizens, were resented. Many were recalled to the Soviet Union, both before and after 1956 when there was a reduction in the number of Russians in North Korea except those directly engaged in technical assistance to industry and to the military establishment.

In general summary of Korean Communist factional experience from 1945 through the post-war period it might be said that shared foreign and domestic experience tended to produce factional political groupings; that in the initial stages of Communist rule the identification of one faction with a predominant foreign Power was the key to hegemony; that identification with a foreign Power in later stages became a political liability; and that changes in the factional balance of power were accompanied by decisions of major economic and social import.

For analytical purposes we have chosen to separate the discussion of intra-party politics from that of inter-party politics with which it is intertwined. To this aspect we now turn.

[9] *Ibid.*

INTER-PARTY POLITICS

> Solidarity centered on the Soviet Union was necessary yesterday, is necessary today, and will be necessary tomorrow. This solidarity around the Soviet Union does not mean that somebody is dominating somebody else; it also does not mean that we are suffering from *sadaejuui* [sycophancy].
>
> Kim Il-song, 1959.[10]

> Although some people say that the Soviet way is best or that the Chinese way is best have we not now reached the point where we can construct our own way?
>
> Kim Il-song, 1955.[11]

While we are not in agreement about the inter-Party political position of the KWP at the end of 1962 (to be explained below), we are in agreement about the following: that the KWP prior to 1950 seemed to be under virtually complete domination by the CPSU; that Chinese involvement in the Korean War made the KWP increasingly responsive to the CPC; that until Korean experimentation with the Chinese agricultural communes in late 1958 the primacy of Soviet control seems to have been maintained; that from 1958 to 1961 there were signs of experimentation with Chinese policies; and that since the Twenty-Second CPSU Congress there has been marked agreement between publicly adopted Korean and Chinese positions on a wide range of issues facing the international Communist movement. Among the latter we would include Sino-Korean agreement on such issues as the treatment of Stalin, Albania, Yugoslavia, Cuba, the Sino-Indian border conflict, and the communes. All of these represent marked divergences from openly adopted Soviet policy positions.

We differ in interpreting the implications of the divergencies. The position of the second writer is that despite these divergencies the KWP cannot but be regarded as a Soviet " puppet " for the following reasons. Kim Il-song and the Kapsan faction owe their ascendancy to Soviet support. They regard the Soviet Union as more powerful than China and as the most advanced model of Communist development. While the Chinese in Korea left a most favourable impression as a wartime ally and as a collaborator in post-war reconstruction, and while there are strong feelings of Sino-Korean cultural affinity, these have not yet brought about a political reorientation from Moscow to Peking. In

10 Kim Il-song, " Choson nodongdang chungang wiwonhoe 1959 nyon 2 wol chonwon hoeuieso han pogo " (" Report at the February 1959 Plenum of the Central Committee of the Korean Workers' Party "), *Selected Works*, VI, pp. 249–250.

11 Kim Il-song, *Sasang saopeso kyojojuuiwa hyongsikchuuirul t'oejihago chuch'erul hwangnip hal te taehayo* (*On Exterminating Dogmatism and Formalism and Establishing Independence in Ideological Work*) (Pyongyang: KWP Press, 1960), p. 12. This passage has been expunged from the version of the speech in the *Selected Works*.

fact, Korean deviations from Soviet positions might be interpreted as a Soviet stratagem by which the C.P.S.U. can keep open communications channels both to China and to Albania in the interests of bloc solidarity under conditions where this becomes difficult for reasons of Soviet national prestige. A compelling argument for the pro-Soviet orientation is that the Korean People's Army is completely Soviet trained and equipped and has only Soviet advisers. Both geography and economic necessity dictate that North Korea depend upon an external Power—the U.S.S.R.

The position of the other writer is that the trend of KWP policy decisions, at least since 1958, no longer makes it accurate to regard the KWP as a Soviet "puppet." [12] Rather the Kapsan leadership has been able to utilise Sino-Soviet differences to enlarge its scope of autonomous action and relies upon the strategic importance of Korea to both giant neighbours in order to avert complete alienation from or domination by either. Although the Chinese have effectively wooed the Koreans through admiring propaganda that they are "proud of" and have "learned from" them, and although the Koreans probably regard the Chinese as their staunchest ally in the event of war, it is unlikely that Communist Korea will accept a modern version of Korea's nineteenth century status as a Chinese tributary state. While the KWP leadership may be pro-Soviet in their general orientation, it is difficult to escape the conclusion that they are anti-Khrushchev. Similarly, the agreements with CPC policy may indicate that the Kapsan faction is not so much pro-Chinese as pro-Mao Tse-tung. The key to KWP behaviour from this point of view is emergent Korean Communist nationalism exemplified in an article published on the occasion of the fiftieth birthday of Kim Il-song in April 1962, which stressed the establishment of *chuch'e* [autonomy, Chinese, *chu-t'i*] by the KWP and mentioned neither Russia nor China.[13]

One of the most interesting events in post-war KWP, CPSU and CPC relations occurred in 1956 immediately after the August Plenum in which many Korean Communists with Russian and Chinese connections were expelled from the KWP. Apparently in the role of an international Communist court of appeal First Deputy Premier Anastas Mikoyan and Marshal P'eng Teh-huai flew secretly to Pyongyang. After hearing the evidence, they apparently advised that the August opposition should not be treated as "anti-Party factionalists" but

[12] See John Bradbury, "Sino-Soviet Competition in North Korea," *The China Quarterly* (April–June 1961), pp. 15–28.

[13] "Ma-k'o-szu-lieh-ning-chu-i cheng-tang tsai wo-kuo ti ch'uang-chien chi-ch'i chuang-ta ho fa-chan" ("The Creation, Strengthening, and Development of a Marxist-Leninist Party in our Country"), *Hsin Ch'ao-hsien* (*New Korea*), No. 4 (162), (1962), pp. 7–12.

should be reinstated in the KWP as loyal critics of Party policy. These decisions were not completely honoured by the Kapsan leadership. A few of those expelled were allowed token readmission to the KWP, but not to former positions of influence. The hunting down and purging of those suspected of harbouring anti-Kim thoughts continued with ruthless vigour. Thus the Chinese Communists apparently had little faith in the Kapsan leadership; they were asked several times to extradite the Yenan-Koreans who had fled to China but they consistently refused.

In its inter-Party relations presumably the KWP leadership will be more attentive to that Party which can ensure its continuance in power and which seems to offer the better prospect for the achievement of Korean unification.

POLITICS OF EXPANSION

> The time has come to unify our country. . . . Forward!
>
> Kim Il-song, June 26, 1950.[14]

> Mr. Chairman and Members of the Supreme Council for National Reconstruction of the Republic of Korea! . . . The Supreme People's Assembly of the Democratic People's Republic of Korea is sending this message to you, appealing to your national conscience, at this critical moment.
>
> Supreme People's Assembly, June 21, 1962.[15]

The extension of Communist power into South Korea under the slogan of " peaceful unification " has been one of the most important objectives of KWP policy in the post-war period. It promises to become an increasingly crucial factor in the future internal and international politics of the Korean Communists.

Although the tragic decision of 1950 to attempt Korean unification by force ended in disaster, the K.W.P. leadership has continued to build and to strengthen a massive military establishment of some 600,000 men in the post-war period. Evidence that they have not ruled out the possibility of forceful unification is provided by a 1955 statement by Kim Il-song that Korea could be unified in either of two ways—" peacefully " or " by war ." Kim specified that the condition for the militant mode of unification would be " a great war on a world scale." Elaborating further, he explained: " Whereas it would be rather difficult for us to fight all alone against American imperialism, under conditions where they must disperse their forces on a global scale it would be

14 *People's Daily*, June 28, 1950, 1.

15 *Message of the Supreme People's Assembly of the Democratic People's Republic of Korea to the Supreme Council for National Reconstruction of the Republic of Korea, the Public and Political Figures and the Entire People of South Korea* (Pyongyang, June 21, 1962), p. 1.

comparatively easy for us to defeat them." [16] Such thinking as this may underly apparent Korean sympathy for the Chinese emphasis upon widespread wars of "national liberation."

The prospect of forfeiting the entire post-war reconstruction effort has not made the renewal of hostilities an attractive policy alternative for the Kapsan faction since the Armistice. Thus they have stressed psychological warfare and subversion. Two classic psychological warfare techniques which they have emphasised have been the tactics of invidious comparison (in which the North is portrayed as heaven and the South as hell) and the tactics of anti-foreignism (in which the American involvement in Korea has been depicted in the most barbarous terms). The Communist psychological offensive against South Korea since 1953 has included offers to send grain to food-short farmers, to provide jobs for all unemployed, to care for all orphans, to establish economic and cultural exchanges, and to set up a federal government in which both northern and southern régimes would continue authority over their respective territories. The current proposal of this type is that "the North and South Korean government authorities conclude an agreement on not attacking the other side by armed force and that the numerical strength of the armies of North and South Korea be cut to 100,000 men or less respectively on condition that the U.S. Army is completely withdrawn from South Korea." [17] The Pyongyang government continues to reject a role for the United Nations in the achievement of Korean unification. There has as yet been no Communist proposal to make South Korea a "neutral zone on the Laos and Cambodian models" such as has been suggested for South Vietnam.

Also in contrast to Vietnam there has been virtually no Communist violence in South Korea during the post-war period. This is to be explained largely on the basis of the strong anti-Communist attitudes developed among the people of the South as a result of the war. Nevertheless, there have been extensive KWP efforts to infiltrate agents and to build an underground organisation for effective political action. This has been particularly difficult since, unlike divided Germany, there has been almost no exchange of persons between North and South since the early phases of the war.

The presence of American military power is regarded by the KWP as the main obstacle to Korean unification. Therefore the principal strategy in South Korea at the present time is to mobilise Korean nationalist sentiments in an anti-American national united front.

[16] Kim Il-song, "Sasang saopeso . . . ," *Selected Works*, IV, p. 343

[17] *Message of the Supreme People's Assembly . . .* , p. 5.

CONCLUSION

In conclusion we wish to point out that Communist politics in North Korea have been characterised by a degree of harshness which it is difficult for an outsider to understand. North Korea fell under Communist rule directly from tight Japanese wartime control which in turn had preserved much of the harsher qualities of nineteenth century Korean Confucianism. The people of North Korea experienced no interlude of freedom which might have helped to set more humane limits to Communist coercion and social psychological manipulation. Thus Communist power sacrificed them to wartime destruction, deprived them of their lands and much of their property, mobilised them as a vast labour army, and drove them to race a Flying Horse into a problematical Communist future.

One indication of the quality of Korean Communist politics is the " cult " of Kim Il-song. At least one high official has been fired from his post because he referred to the KWP leader as *tongmu* (the ordinary word for " comrade ") rather than *t'ongji* (the honorific form). This aspect of North Korean Communism may help to explain the Kapsan faction's lack of interest in emulating Khrushchev's anti-Stalin campaign. If anything the idolisation and deification of Kim Il-song has increased in intensity since 1956. The experience of Korea, as that of China, thus suggests that the continued sanctification of a charismatic leader may be a necessary correlate of the Communist transformation of an underdeveloped country.

In retrospect, the post-war period has seen the rise of the Kapsan faction to real power, the emergence of the KWP from complete subordination to the CPSU (although debatable in extent and direction), the growth of Chinese influence, and the intensification of hostility against the American presence in the Republic of Korea. The dominance of the Kapsan faction and the unchallenged authority of the KWP indicate that a considerable degree of political stability has been achieved in contemporary North Korea. This consolidation of political power, accompanied by economic development and social change, presents a number of perplexing questions for the future of Communist Korea. Will the KWP attempt to build a powerful " socialist industrial-agricultural state " be successful in its objective of exerting a strong pull on the political sympathies of the people of South Korea? Will Sino-Soviet differences eventually force the KWP into an open break with one of its giant neighbours? Will reactivation of latent factional animosities take place in connection with pressures for inter-Party alignment? Will the KWP again turn to violence, perhaps with Chinese encouragement as a method for Korean unification?

Some of the ominous ambiguities of contemporary Korean Communist politics can be illustrated by the single word *insa* (which can mean either " greetings " or " personnel ") which Kim Il-song employed in his speech of August 15, 1960. Said Kim: " On the occasion of the fifteenth anniversary of Liberation, on behalf of the Korean Workers' Party and the Government of the Republic, I send to the South Korean people, who are struggling heroically against the American imperialists and their running-dogs, militant *insa* and the warm support and encouragement of the people of the North." [18]

[18] Kim Il-song, *Choson inminui minjokchok myongjol 8.15 haebang 15 chunyon kyongch'uk taehoeeso han pogo (Report at the Meeting to Celebrate the 15th Anniversary of the August 15 Liberation, the Great National Holiday of the Korean People)*, (Pyongyang: KWP Press, 1960), p. 27.

The Foreign Policy of North Korea

By ROBERT A. SCALAPINO

ON October 23, 1962, Premier Kim Il-song outlined the foreign policy of his government before the Supreme People's Assembly, meeting in Pyongyang.[1] His lengthy speech, entitled "Immediate Tasks of the Democratic People's Republic of Korea," ranged over both domestic and foreign policy issues. To set forth the major themes of that speech is a convenient method of introducing the foreign policy of North Korea.

Kim made the transition from domestic to foreign policy by discussing the question of Korean unification, and the role of the United States in South Korea. The Communist position on the American role in Korea was succinctly stated in the following passage:

> The occupation of South Korea by the U.S. imperialists and their aggressive policy are the root cause of all the misfortunes and sufferings of the South Korean people, and the main obstacle to the progress of South Korean society and peaceful unification of the country.[2]

Having thus depicted the United States as Public Enemy Number 1, Kim continued by painting South Korean conditions in the blackest possible hues. The economy of the South is "totally ruined," he asserted. National industry, "under the pressure of U.S. monopoly capital and comprador capital" is completely bankrupt. Unemployment affects 60 per cent. of the population. Agriculture is also in desperate straits. "The broad peasant masses are still being harshly exploited under the feudalistic landlord system."[3] Moreover, South Korean lives and property "are being constantly threatened by the American robbers." According to Kim, rape, murder and pillage by foreign usurpers are rampant.

It would be fascinating to know to what extent Kim's listeners and readers accept this standard Communist picture of the South. Do they suspect gross exaggeration and distortion? Do they ever wonder why so few South Koreans flee this hell-hole for the North? Are they puzzled that anti-American incidents are few and generally of minor proportions?

1 For an English translation of portions of this speech, see "Premier Kim Il-song Makes Speech on Immediate Tasks of DPRK Government," *The People's Korea*, No. 88, October 31, 1962, pp. 1–7.
2 *Ibid.* p. 6.
3 *Ibid.* p. 6.

Kim proceeded to set forth the orthodox Communist proposals for gradual unification of North and South. The Korean question, he maintained, must be settled by the Koreans themselves. The United Nations, party to aggression, could not be involved. The first step in unification would be the removal of American forces from Korea, a peace agreement between North and South stipulating no military attack upon each other, and the reduction of the armed forces of each side to 100,000 men or less. Economic and cultural co-operation would also be initiated. The next step would be a confederation, with a supreme national committee composed of representatives of the governments of both sides. This committee would be empowered to solve " jointly " matters of common concern, but would leave the present socio-political systems of North and South untouched, thus ensuring the independent activities of the two governments. Ultimately, out of confederation would come a unified central government " representing all strata " of Koreans, elected by " free all-Korea elections on democratic principles." [4]

In concluding his remarks about unification, Kim repeated the appeal for all Korean patriots to " smash decisively the policy of national split pursued by the U.S. imperialists and rally themselves closely under the banner of the anti-American, national salvation struggle, under the banner of the unification of the country."

The next topic discussed by the Premier was relations between North Korea and its " fraternal Socialist allies." Kim's basic theme, taken from the Moscow Statement of 1960, was that "the forces of peace and Socialism are overpowering the forces of war and imperialism in the world arena." [5] There followed a cautiously worded and carefully balanced appraisal of Soviet and Chinese accomplishments. Homage was paid first to the Soviet people:

> The great Soviet people are pioneering the highway to Communism, the ideal for mankind. The Soviet Union is carrying on grand economic construction for laying a material and technical basis of Communism, and the welfare of the working people in the Soviet Union is further improving. The Soviet Union is leading the world in the scientific and technological development and is registering ever greater achievements in this sphere.[6]

Tribute to the Chinese people followed immediately:

> The fraternal Chinese people, courageously overcoming all difficulties, are making great exploits in their Socialist construction in the course of their forward march. Despite all sorts of calumny and slander by the imperialists and world reactionaries, the Chinese People's Republic stands firm in the heart of Asia as a great Socialist power and its international influence is further growing.[7]

[4] *Ibid.* p. 6. [5] *Ibid.* pp. 6–7 [6] *Ibid.* p. 7. [7] *Ibid.* p. 7.

The Socialist camp, Kim asserted, has the primary and immediate task of helping the peoples of colonial and dependent areas to gain national liberation and defeat imperialism. The imperialist forces, led by the United States, will stop at nothing, according to Kim, to oppose Socialist objectives and to unleash a new war. Thus no struggle for peace can be conducted apart from a fight against the United States. The catalogue of American crimes is a lengthy one. American actions relating to NATO, West Germany, Cuba, South Korea, South Vietnam, Japan and Taiwan are all cited as proof that American policy is directed towards aggression and war. There follows one of the most interesting passages in Kim's entire speech:

> Peace is not to be begged for, but must be won through the struggle of the popular masses. We can avert a new world war and maintain a durable world peace only by steadily reinforcing the might of the Socialist camp, further developing the Labour movement in the capitalist countries and the liberation struggle of the peoples of the colonial and dependent countries . . . only by bringing pressure to bear upon the imperialist war-incendiaries and dealing them blows everywhere, by firmly rallying all the peace forces and combining all methods of struggle.[8]

It should be remembered that the Indian and Cuban crises were rapidly developing at the time when these words were uttered. If one major enemy of peace is the United States, according to Kim, the other is modern revisionism. " The modern revisionists represented by the Tito clique of Yugoslavia are faithfully serving U.S. imperialism, attempting to undermine the unity of the Socialist camp, defend the aggressive manoeuvres of imperialism and paralyse the revolutionary struggle of the popular masses."[9] The revisionists are slandering the Socialist countries and engineering plots to set them against each other, even to overthrow the parties and governments of these countries. Thus the fight against revisionism must be continued with vigour.

The DPRK government and people, asserted Kim, have one basic policy with respect to their Socialist comrades: to consolidate and protect the unity of the Socialist camp, by firmly adhering to Marxist-Leninist norms of conduct. " Today our country has established an indestructible alliance with our great neighbours, the Soviet Union and the People's Republic of China, under the Treaty of Friendship, Co-operation and Mutual Assistance concluded with each of them."[10]

Finally, Kim made some remarks directed particularly toward the Afro-Asian " neutralist " world:

> Our country regards it as the consistent line of its foreign policy to establish, on the principle of peaceful coexistence with the countries of

[8] *Ibid.* p. 7.
[9] *Ibid.* p. 7.
[10] *Ibid.* p. 7.

> differing social systems, normal state relations with all the countries which respect the freedom and independence of our people, and especially to develop relations of friendly co-operation with the national-independent countries in Asia, Africa and Latin America.[11]

Foreign Policy Organs

From the above remarks can be discerned the main lines of North Korean foreign policy as expressed by the most authoritative voice of the régime. Before analysing these remarks further and providing certain background information, let us note briefly the foreign policy mechanism, as it exists and operates in North Korea. As in most other societies, Communist and non-Communist, the Ministry of Foreign Affairs is not perhaps of central importance in the making of foreign policy. Nevertheless, it plays a significant role in assembling the data upon which policy is based, and in transmitting and administering policy once it has been established. The present Foreign Minister is Pak Song-chol, also a leading KWP member. Currently, North Korea has embassies in the eleven bloc countries, and it is interesting to note that in five of these, namely Albania, China, East Germany, North Vietnam and the U.S.S.R., the North Korean ambassador is a member of the Central Committee of the Korean Workers' Party. Clearly, these posts are considered of special importance. In addition to representation in the bloc countries, DPRK embassies also exist in Algeria, Cuba, Guinea and Mali. Consular posts are maintained in Rangoon, Djakarta, Cairo and New Delhi. At this stage, official North Korean representation is fairly limited outside the bloc.

A much wider coverage is obtained, however, through other channels. Like the Chinese Communists, the North Koreans maintain a number of organisations that serve as adjuncts or supplements to official diplomatic agencies. For example, the Korean Committee for Cultural Relations with Foreign Countries is used to bring individuals and groups from various countries, many of which have no official relations with North Korea. The Korean Committee for Asian and African Solidarity organises activities appropriate to its name, sends representatives to various international conferences, and seeks to keep in general touch with the Afro-Asian world. There are other organisations of a " special function " or " special interest " nature such as the Korean National Peace Committee and the Korean Democratic Youth League. In Japan, thousands of Korean residents are enrolled in the General Association of Korean Residents in Japan, an organisation controlled completely by the Korean Workers' Party.

[11] *Ibid.* p. 7.

Thus, in July 1961, *Rodong Sinmun* heralded the widening contacts of North Korea, claiming that the DPRK government had trade relations with forty countries and commercial treaties with ten countries besides the Socialist bloc; maintained cultural relations with seventy countries (counting various individuals and groups brought to Korea from various areas of the world); and belonged to some fifty international organisations.[12] In fact, of course, many of these trade and cultural relations were on a very small scale. Nevertheless, they represented the bid for world recognition and support that now characterises North Korean foreign policy.

In any Communist society, the Party is the supreme decision-making body, and those men who lead the Party—men in the Central Committee, or more precisely, in the Politburo—hold the key policy-making positions. It is men like Choe Yong-kon, Kim Il, Pak Kum-chol, Kim Chang-man, and Yi Hyo-sun who can speak authoritatively on foreign policy issues. But it must never be forgotten that Kim Il-song is currently in a position of complete supremacy. Whatever, the covert opposition to him, Kim now reigns without fear of serious rivalry. He has swept away the opposition that once existed, and at present there is only the Kim faction, at least at the top. The adulation given Kim by the mass media is extraordinary. If ever a cult of personality existed under Communism, it exists in North Korea today. Hence, Kim Il-song is the most powerful voice on issues of foreign as well as domestic policy. For North Korea, this is a Stalinist age, and Kim is the all-conquering, all-wise hero to whom everyone must pay homage.

The manipulation of North Korean public opinion on behalf of the positions of the régime follows standard Communist practice. Mass rallies are organised " to denounce American imperialism in Cuba " or " to protest against ROK-Japan treaty talks." Occasionally, they are conducted for positive purposes—to welcome a visiting Chinese delegation or " to support world peace." Sometimes, these rallies or meetings are under the auspices of one of the organisations noted above; sometimes, they are directed by the KWP itself. In Japan, similar activities are conducted by Korean associations connected with the DPRK government.

POLICY TOWARDS SOUTH KOREA AND THE U.S.

Let us return to the substantive elements in North Korean foreign policy, advancing beyond the brief outline sketched by Premier Kim in his October speech. First, what is the basic policy of the DPRK towards the Republic of Korea, and towards the United States? In

[12] *Rodong Sinmun* (*Labour News*), July 2, 1961, p. 1.

discussing these matters, several key factors must be kept in mind, factors well known to the Communists. The population of the North is only one-half of that in the South. Like East Germany, North Korea would have no hope of dominating a unified nation unless the KWP could win substantial support from South Koreans. But despite the very real problems of the South, there is extremely limited support for Communism among South Koreans at present, irrespective of age, occupation or social status.

Hence the North cannot and will not accept any concept of unification involving nationwide free elections. It also rejects the United Nations both because it sees the U.N. as a projection of American policy with respect to Korea and because it knows that internationally supervised elections at this time would result in Communist defeat and subordination to a non-Communist government. The idea of confederation is, of course, designed to protect the autonomy and integrity of a government and party that would be a distinct minority element in any truly unified Korea.

Basically, the tactics and strategy of the North Korean Communists are similar to those of the North Vietnamese Communists.[13] The Communist leaders of North Korea hope to see the development of a "Liberation Front," a political-military movement in South Korea dedicated to the support of the Communist unification plan, and operating as a broad nationalist-Communist alliance. At present, the Communists are seeking to lay the political groundwork for such a movement, since conditions are not ripe for any type of military operations. Propaganda of all kinds, including a Marxist-Leninist "University of the Air," is beamed southward. If the DPRK authorities are successful in launching grass-roots organisations or movements in the South, at some point, they would open up a struggle phase, as has been done in South Vietnam. Cadres from the North would be filtered down to lead their southern compatriots, with peasant-based guerrilla warfare gradually extended.

The themes for this campaign have already been spelled out in very clear fashion. The central struggle is to capture the nationalist movement, the quest of the Communists everywhere in Asia. While the North successfully builds Socialism, the South must mobilise all its patriotic people for an anti-American, National Liberation Front. This Front must oust foreign imperialism and press for democratic reforms, preliminary steps to joining, the Socialist North. "The Fascist clique

[13] There has been no Communist proposal for the neutralisation of South Korea, as in the case of South Vietnam, but the insistence upon the removal of American forces aims towards the same basic objective.

led by Pak Chung-hi " must naturally be toppled, and replaced by " progressive " leadership.

It is natural that the North Korean leaders, like the leaders of North Vietnam, would see the United States as primary enemy, central obstacle to Communist success. Since the inauguration of the DPRK, the United States has been the great *bête noire.* The inability of the Communist Party to survive in the South, and the anaemic character of the United Front or National Liberation movement, the failure of the Communist military thrust in 1950 (naturally proclaimed an act of ROK-American aggression), and the very existence of the Republic of Korea are blamed essentially upon the United States.

DPRK leaders believe that the United States is dedicated first to the isolation of North Korea and finally to its destruction. They see the United States as providing the primary impetus for an alliance involving Japan, South Korea and Taiwan, aimed at the Communist world. This alliance, they believe, would ultimately be political and military in character as well as economic. The charge that America is fostering a North-East Asian Treaty Organisation is constantly reiterated by North Korean leaders. Moreover, the Communists recognise that as American power frustrated their military moves in an earlier era, that power would also be used to thwart revolutionary victory, should conditions in the South become propitious for guerrilla warfare, as in South Vietnam. In a broader sense, of course, Korean Communist leaders, like their counterparts in China and Vietnam, see the United States as their most powerful and dangerous opponent, encircling them with bases, threatening them with measures that range from extensive economic-political pressures to atomic war. For North Korean spokesmen, therefore " the struggle for peace," as noted earlier, is inseparable from " the fight against American imperialism."

It is difficult to exaggerate the vituperative character of North Korean assaults upon the United States. The following quotation, while a rather extreme example, is not unique:

> The " American way of life " is characterised by its egoistic mammonism, fostered by private ownership of the bourgeoisie in the course of their competition and by its immorality, depravity, degeneration and medieval bestiality and cruelty. The atrocities of American soldiers in South Korea, who kill a three-year-old child on the charge of " theft," madly drive cars over passers-by and violate and kill young women, expose for all to see the true colour of the two-legged beasts educated in the " American way of life " and devoid of a trace of conscience and humanity.
>
> The " American way of life " is the most shameless and degenerate way of life of the ugliest, most barefaced and bestial cannibals, with no precedent in the East and West, and is an ideological-moral weapon to insure the exploitation and plunder by the monopoly capitalists and

the annihilation of the working people and small nations which are weak politically and economically.[14]

Clearly, this is the Asian counterpart of the Yellow Peril, with some added Marxist trappings. One senses a strong element of traditional anti-Westernism reminiscent of the era when Korea was rightly called the Hermit Kingdom. Some of the charges almost parallel those that were current in the nineteenth century, when missionaries were accused of slaughtering babies for medical or experimental purposes. Yet this is also a part of the new nationalism, the continuous, purposeful drive of the Communists to make nationalism a supreme weapon on their behalf.

North Korea, Russia and China

To combat the American threat, real and imagined, North Korea must have allies. Currently, as would be expected, her foremost allies are the Soviet Union and Communist China, each committed to her through bilateral treaties. These two treaties, ratified only a few days apart, symbolise North Korean commitment, security—and, currently, its major foreign policy dilemma as well. The Treaty of Friendship, Co-operation and Mutual Assistance between the U.S.S.R. and the DPRK was signed on July 6, 1961, at the Kremlin. A top-drawer North Korean delegation headed by Kim Il-song himself was present. In speeches for the occasion, Kim and Khrushchev sought to strike common notes: the menace of American imperialism in Asia, the great progress of the Communist world, and its unbreakable unity. " We can confidently say," remarked Khrushchev, " that never in the history of mankind have there been parties which could achieve such unity as the Communist and workers' parties have established today." [15]

Kim and party proceeded directly to Peking where on July 11 a very similar Treaty was concluded with the Chinese People's Republic. A joint Korean-Chinese communique issued at the time made the following significant points:

1. Both parties would remain " consistently and unswervingly faithful " to the Moscow Declaration of 1957 and the Moscow Statement of 1960, documents given strong emphasis.

2. " The two parties were of the common view that modern revisionism represented by the leading group of Yugoslavia was the main danger to the present international Communist movement, and that a resolute struggle must be waged against it."

[14] An article in the *Minju Choson*, July 24, 1962, as reported by Pyongyang Radio, July 26, 1962.

[15] Khrushchev's speech as reported in *The People's Korea*, No. 24, July 12, 1961, p. 2.

3. " The two parties pointed out that Korea and China consistently pursued a foreign policy of peace and made unremitting efforts for the realisation of peaceful coexistence among nations with different social systems and relaxation of international tension.

4. " The two parties pointed out with stress that U.S. imperialism, the common enemy of the people of the world, is stepping up in an all-round way its aggressive activities and war preparations . . . the whole world must continue to maintain a high degree of vigilance." [16]

Upon his return to Pyongyang on July 15, Premier Kim spoke at a rally of 300,000 citizens. The speech reads as if the author had carefully measured each phrase, each word, so as to give the Soviet Union and China absolutely equal billing. Nevertheless, careful scrutiny of the substance of the speeches and communiques in Moscow and Peking suggests that North Korea was already having some difficulties in maintaining its neutral stance in the face of a growing cleavage between Mao and Khrushchev. The Kremlin speeches certainly cover the basic ground " correctly " in a formal sense. They tend to lack the qualities of intimacy characteristic of the Peking statements, however, and the vocabulary used is more restrained. In Peking, Kim gave unstinting praise to Chinese leadership, asserting that their successful construction of Socialism was consolidating the power of the whole Socialist camp, and of particular encouragement to the peoples of Asia, Africa and Latin America in their struggle for peace, national independence and social progress. He proclaimed that " No power on earth can destroy this friendship and solidarity between our two peoples." And Chou En-lai answered in kind: " China and Korea are real brothers in a big family of Socialism, and friendship between the two peoples is a tested one through bitter struggles." [17]

The Sino-Soviet Dispute

Nearly two years have passed since those words were spoken. These have been years of increasing strain for the Sino-Soviet alliance, with sharp repercussions throughout the Communist world. It may well be that for the moment at least, the problem of the crisis within the bloc supersedes the problem of " American imperialism " in so far as DPRK leaders are concerned. To understand the North Korean position—and the dilemma—it is necessary to trace briefly events since that time. When Khrushchev openly attacked the Albanian leaders at the 22nd CPSU Congress in October 1961 and provoked an angry retort from

[16] *Ibid.* No. 25, July 19, 1961, p. 1; see also *Peking Review*, No. 28, July 14, 1961, pp. 5–7.

[17] Premier Chou En-lai's speech as reported in *The People's Korea*, No. 25, *op. cit.*, p. 2.

Chou En-lai, Kim and the Korean delegation remained publicly silent. In his speech before the Congress, Kim neither criticised Albania nor did he belabour the evils of Stalinism, despite what must have been substantial Soviet pressure to do so.

The tactics of "neutralism" were further advanced in early November. On November 7, less than a week after the Korean delegation had returned to Pyongyang, the KWP sent a telegram of effusive praise to the Soviet Union on the occasion of the 44th anniversary of the successful October Revolution. The following day, however, a slightly less reverent but entirely positive message was sent to the Albanian leaders on the occasion of the 20th anniversary of the founding of the Albanian Workers' Party. The KWP praised the achievements of the Albanian Workers' Party, both in the war of liberation and in the tasks of Socialist construction, and concluded with the statement: "We firmly believe that the friendship and solidarity between the peoples of Albania and Korea will continue to develop and become stronger in the future under the principles of Marxism-Leninism and proletarian internationalism—within the great family of the Socialist camp headed by the U.S.S.R." [18] This tactic of "mutual recognition," incidentally, was followed by a number of other Asian Communist Parties.[19]

On November 27, Premier Kim reported on the 22nd CPSU Congress to the Enlarged Plenum of the 4th KWP Central Committee. His speech contained eulogistic praise of Soviet progress. "Today," he asserted, "Communism no longer remains a mere ideal but is turning into reality in the Soviet Union, the first Socialist state. . . . There is no doubt that the new CPSU programme and its fulfilment will have a powerful impact on drawing hundreds of millions of people the world over to the side of Communism." [20]

Kim pronounced the CPSU "the commonly recognised vanguard of the international Communist movement." By this, he made it clear, he was referring to an historic fact: the U.S.S.R. represented the first society where the Communist Party achieved power, and hence the society that had pioneered Socialism.

His comments upon de-Stalinisation were brief and somewhat guarded. He said: "At the Congress, much mention was made of the cult of Stalin's personality. This problem arose from the internal party life of the CPSU. The problem of anti-Party factionalist elements was also discussed. Stalin was a leader of the international Communist movement, and his influence in the movement was great. The name of

[18] *Rodong Sinmun*, November 8, 1961, p. 1.

[19] For some details, see my article, "Moscow, Peking and the Communist Parties of Asia," *Foreign Affairs*, January 1963, pp. 323–343

[20] *Rodong Sinmun* carried the full text of this speech on pp. 1–2 of its November 28, 1961, issue.

Stalin is well known among the Communists and the people of the entire world. However, as far as Stalin is concerned, the Soviet Communist Party members should know him better than anyone else. The problem of how to evaluate Stalin's activities in the U.S.S.R. belongs to the category of intra-Party problems of the CPSU. The problem of anti-Party factionalists is also a problem entirely within the boundary of internal CPSU problems. We recognise that no Party can interfere in the internal affairs of any of its brotherly Parties. This is one of the basic principles to which all brotherly Parties must adhere in their relations with each other. Therefore, the problem of Stalin and anti-Party factions in the CPSU has nothing to do with our party and cannot be a subject of discussion by or in our Party. We can only rejoice in the fact and believe that all people should rally around their own Party Central Committee and carry out their own revolutionary tasks."

Reference to Albania followed immediately. Kim reported that recently, relations between the CPSU and the AWP had become "abnormal," and despite various discussions at the Congress, these relations were becoming even more complicated. "If this continues," asserted Kim, "it will result in serious losses to the unity of the Socialist camp and to the strength of the international Communist movement, and can only benefit our enemies." He continued: "Our Party sincerely hopes that this problem will be solved on the basis of proletarian internationalism and the interests of the international Communist movement, with patient efforts made to settle existing difficulties between the CPSU and Albania."

Throughout this significant speech, great emphasis was placed upon the preservation of solidarity within the Socialist camp against all imperialist and revisionist assaults. The themes of complete equality and independence for each party were repeatedly underscored. And a strong insistence upon unanimity in connection with decision-making in accordance with the Moscow agreements was made.

One day later, on November 28, on the occasion of the 17th anniversary of the liberation of Albania, the KWP sent another warm message of congratulations to the Albanian leaders, remarking upon "the correct leadership of the AWP" who had overcome mounting difficulties bravely and were steadily strengthening the nation's Socialist development.[21] The message praised the Albanian people for having "exposed and destroyed at each step the imperialists and their lackeys, the Yugosalv revisionists," thereby "fighting to defend the great achievements of Socialism."

In the months that followed, North Korean leaders continued to take a "neutralist" stance in public. Throughout this period, intense

[21] See *Rodong Sinmun*, November 29, 1961, p. 1, for the official message.

manoeuvering was taking place, with figures like Ho Chi Minh seeking to serve as mediators in the great East-West split that was threatening the international Communist movement. No doubt, the worried Communist leaders of Asia, including Kim Il-song, applied maximum pressure upon Moscow and Peking to reconcile their differences lest the quarrel split every Communist Party in the world and wreak havoc with Communist unity and strength. A lull in the Sino-Soviet storm did take place in the spring of 1962. Public criticisms within the bloc subsided, and eulogies of Albania from the East ceased to pour forth. Other signs of quiescence developed—but no resolution of the basic issues appeared to be in sight. At most, this era represented an earnest attempt to limit the tactics of dispute, to play for time and avoid any further escalation of conflict.

Despite the lull, moreover, Communist China and the Soviet Union continued to campaign for support throughout the Communist world. Public missions sallied forth, debate at international conferences continued, and in addition, there may well have been far more intricate—and deadly—struggles taking place within and between Communist Party hierarchies. In this setting, can one discern any new trend with respect to the North Korean position? Certainly up to September 1962, the signs were minimal. It can be noted perhaps that the North Koreans were being wooed the more ardently by Peking, and responding the more warmly. In late April, a mission from the CPR national People's Congress headed by P'eng Chen arrived in North Korea, invited by the Supreme People's Assembly. The public exchange of messages was used to testify to the unbreakable solidarity of the Sino-Korean alliance. P'eng said: "The great friendship sealed between our two peoples with blood on the basis of Marxism-Leninism will shine forever." Later, Pak Kum-ch'ol, vice-chairman of the KWP Central Committee responded with these words: "We regard the friendship with the great Chinese people as a most precious thing that cannot be exchanged for anything." [22] Had anyone—let us say Khrushchev—suggested an exchange? In June, the Koreans reciprocated by sending a mission to China headed by Pak. Once again, an atmosphere of great cordiality and agreement was conveyed.

Various occasions in the summer of 1962 were also used to reaffirm the friendship and alliance between the Soviet Union and the DPRK government. At the time of Kim Il-song's 50th birthday in April, Moscow sent greetings; on the first anniversary of the signing of the Soviet-Korean Treaty in early July, speeches pledging continuous and unbreakable friendship were made; on the occasion of the 17th anniversary of the August 15 Liberation of Korea, messages and speeches

[22] *The People's Korea*, No. 63, May 9, 1962, p. 1.

were again exchanged, reiterating the theme of "everlasting and immortal friendship." One detects, however, a certain formalism and lack of spontaneity in the public communications flowing between Moscow and Pyongyang during this period, as if a dance of duty were being performed. Certainly, the vocabulary used is more restrained than that characterising Sino-Korean exchanges.

The Indian and Cuban Crises

In the autumn of 1962, relations between Moscow and Peking clearly worsened, and North Korean "neutralism" was put to new and strenuous tests. The immediate issues were Yugoslavia, India and Cuba. And on all of these issues Pyongyang lined up with Peking. In the face of Khrushchev's persistent efforts to woo Tito, and bring Yugoslavia back into the fold, North Korean spokesmen, in company with their Chinese comrades, continued a running attack upon "the Tito revisionist clique." Even as the Soviet President Brezhnev visited Belgrade, the North Koreans denounced Yugoslavia in unmeasured terms. Pyongyang Radio said on September 25: "The Tito revisionist clique, traitors to the international Communist movement and faithful lackeys of U.S. imperialism, have reduced Yugoslavia to an appendage of imperialism politically and economically." [23] The attack was intensified as Tito prepared for his Moscow journey. On November 17, *Rodong Sinmun* lashed out at revisionists, no longer indentifying them merely as Titoists: "While making all-out efforts for distorting the principles of Marxism-Leninism to deprive it of revolutionary spirit, modern revisionists, as ideological hirelings of U.S. imperalism, are unhesitatingly pursuing, at the imperialists' instigation, their vicious policy of slandering and dividing the Socialist countries, in an attempt to overthrow the parties and governments of these countries.

"Therefore, all the Marxist-Leninists should always be on the alert against all the subversive activities by these revisionists, and struggle to smash them into smithereens." [24] It appeared that Premier Khrushchev himself was being brought under direct attack.

Not only upon the issue of revisionism, but also in connection with the immediate crises of India and Cuba, Peking had no stauncher public ally than Pyongyang. North Korean organs launched a vigorous campaign against the Nehru government shortly after the intensified border struggle erupted in October 1961. The Indian leaders were condemned

[23] Pyongyang Radio, September 26, 1962.

[24] See the significant *Rodong Sinmun* editorial, "Let's hold aloft the Revolutionary Banner of Marxism-Leninism," November 17, 1962, an abridged translation of which is carried in *The People's Korea*, No. 92, November 28, 1962, p. 2.

as " reactionaries " working hand in glove with the American imperialists, helping them to use the Sino-Indian boundary dispute for their sinister purposes. It was asserted that the Indians had begun to nibble at Chinese territory as early as 1951, and had mistaken the Chinese efforts for peace as a sign of weakness. Finally, they had launched a large-scale attack against China, and the CPR government had had no choice except to take self-defence measures in order to check the reckless aggression spearheaded by Indian reactionary circles.[25] As noted earlier, North Korean leaders took a strongly militant position on the Cuban problem: the appeasement of American imperialism does not pay. Supporting Castro " without qualification," the North Koreans exhorted all friends of peace and Socialism to stand firm, forcing the U.S. imperialists to take their " bloodstained hands off Cuba at once." [26]

" Neutralism " in the Sino-Soviet Dispute

As 1962 came to a close, the DPRK government faced a serious problem with respect to bloc relations. The Sino-Soviet cleavage was steadily worsening, and an open break between the two Communist giants could no longer be considered a remote prospect. At the very least, long-range, serious differences were going to continue between Moscow and Peking, and the struggle for power and influence within the Communist and neutralist worlds was going to become more intense. The Korean Workers' Party, in company with many other Asian Communist Parties, had sought to pursue a " neutralist " or non-aligned position between Russia and China, meanwhile exerting all possible pressure to close the gap. Perhaps the techniques of neutralism can be outlined as follows:

1. Approximately equal space is to be given the Soviet Union and Communist China, and equally laudatory terms are to be used in describing the accomplishments of these two societies. In any listing of " fraternal Socialist allies," the U.S.S.R. is normally mentioned first, followed by the Chinese People's Republic, and then the other Communist states. Moreover, the CPSU is recognised on occasion as the " vanguard " or " centre " of the international Communist movement. These actions constitute recognition of the prior existence, the major strength, and the historic leadership role of the Soviet Union. They do not necessarily indicate approval for the current policies or leadership of the CPSU.

25 See the statement issued November 23, 1962, by the DPRK government, partly translated in *ibid.* p. 1.

26 See speeches made at the Pyongyang rally of October 26, 1962, as reported in *ibid.* No. 89, November 7, 1962, p. 2.

2. Only complimentary terms are to be used about "fraternal Socialist allies" in public, and the emphasis is to be upon the unbreakable solidarity of the *twelve* members of the bloc (Albania included). Great stress is placed upon abiding by the Moscow agreements of 1957 and 1960, using these as guide-lines for policy and the settlement of differences within the bloc. One theme constantly reiterated is that all members of the Communist Commonwealth are completely free and equal, and that policy decisions should be reached by the process of discussion, consensus and unanimity. Another theme, increasingly in evidence, is that there must be no interference in the internal affairs of another party.

3. Yugoslavia is to be severely attacked. Tito is to be regarded as a running-dog of Western imperialism, an anti-Marxist-Leninist and a disrupter of the unity of the Socialist camp. Revisionism in general is to be regarded as the primary danger inside the Socialist world, and American imperialism outside that world. Both must be crushed. Primary emphasis is to be given to *the struggle* for peace, support by all possible methods for the national liberation movements, and resolute opposition to every imperialist "manoeuvre."

The phenomenon of "neutralism" within the Communist world has thus far been confined essentially to Eastern Asia. It encompasses the Communist movements of such countries as North Korea, North Vietnam, Indonesia, Japan, Burma, Malaya and Thailand. But as the Soviet Union and Communist China continue to drift apart, and an open split is threatened, "neutralism" becomes a much more difficult tactic to execute successfully. The pressures to force commitment either to one side or to the other mount, both internally and externally. Perhaps North Korea is the foremost example of a Communist state that has now committed itself on a wide series of issues to a pro-Peking position, as noted earlier.

Background to the Peking-Pyongyang Axis

It is appropriate here to suggest some of the fundamental causative factors for the North Korean drift toward Communist China. In the first place, the history of the Korean Communist movement—and of Kim Il-song—is considerably more complex than has generally been realised. Chinese influence has been fairly substantial. As a young man, Kim himself first participated in the Chinese Communist movement, operating in Manchuria. When he and his guerrilla fighters were finally pushed into Siberia as a result of Japanese pressure in 1941, he transferred his membership to the Soviet Communist Party, and later, in 1945, he entered Korea with Soviet troops in the uniform of a Red

Army major. However, Kim was not a "Made in Russia" Communist in the same sense as the Russianised Koreans who also arrived with the Red Army and many of whom were born in the Soviet Union or had lived most of their lives there.

Moreover, it was the Russia of Stalin that gave Kim his initial opportunities, not the Russia of Nikita Khrushchev. There is little question that without Soviet support, Kim could not have triumphed over his multiple rivals in the troubled early years after 1945. Indeed, without that support, in all probability, he would not have been a serious contender for power. If Russia provided indispensable assistance in this era, however, it also provided problems. Basically, Kim had to defend his power against both the so-called Moscow and Yenan factions, as well as against the previously existing indigenous Communist and nationalist groups. It is significant that in 1956, Kim's internal opponents were charging him with a cult of personality and other crimes of a Stalinist character. And, of course, these charges, derived from the exposé of the 20th CPSU Congress, were true. Kim's troubles in this period (despite the fact that they involved mainly Yenan faction men) could scarcely have endeared Khrushchev to him.

It has ultimately been the Kim faction that has triumphed in North Korea over all other factions. After a lengthy series of purges, only those men personally loyal to Kim have remained on top, a number of them old guerrilla fighters with him. Non-alignment is one expression of nationalism in foreign policy, as the neutralist world has long demonstrated. Clearly, this same force of nationalism began to figure more prominently in the foreign policy of North Korea as Kim and his cohorts gradually acquired political supremacy and some measure of security.

In addition, it must be understood that the Soviet record in postwar Korea generally suffers in comparison with that of the Chinese Communists. Russian troops behaved very badly when they first came into North Korea. Pillage, rape and other crimes were widespread, and Soviet troops quickly made themselves hated and feared among the populace. Chinese troops, on the other hand, were relatively well disciplined at the time of the Korean War, and established much better rapport with the citizenry according to most accounts. Moreover, the Korean Communist élite were naturally aware of the fact that it was the Chinese, not the Russians who had risked everything to keep North Korea Communist. The repeated emphasis upon phrases such as "our friendship has been forged and tested in blood," suggests that this act has not been forgotten by either the Chinese or the North Koreans. Perhaps some leaders in Pyongyang suspect that such help might be needed again. Finally, in recent years, Chinese economic assistance and technical aid to North Korea appears to have been more important than Russian aid, despite the problems faced by Peking. Both in war and peace, the Chinese have sacrificed more for their "fraternal brothers."

These facts, in turn, suggest some broader considerations. It is, of course, important that Korea lies within the historic sphere of Chinese cultural and political influence. China, as an emergent, dynamic force, would cast a long shadow over Asia in this era, whatever its ideological and political commitments. In times of Chinese power, Korea was always profoundly affected. It must be remembered that while Korea shares borders with both the U.S.S.R. and Communist China, Peking is relatively close, Moscow is far away.

Perhaps it is more important, however, that North Korea shares a timing of revolution with China, and hence, a relatively similar world outlook. The Communist leaders of both societies represent a first-generation revolutionary élite, essentially intellectual in character, accustomed to think and act in militant terms, profoundly dissatisfied with world conditions, and holding a deeply anti-Western bias, compounded out of nationalism, Marxism-Leninism and historic xenophobia. Like the early Bolsheviks, these élites cannot think of successfully challenging the United States directly, in terms of economic or military competition. Instead, they must support a rolling revolution in the non-Western world in the hope that its success will effectively and quickly weaken America. This is the shortcut to competition with the United States, one with many risks but at the same time attractive to those who feel themselves surrounded, frustrated, and possibly imperilled by American power. It is not surprising that the North Koreans see the world more in accordance with Chinese than with Russian views.

It must also be noted that Soviet diplomacy under Khrushchev, as under Stalin, has had many of the hallmarks of "big power chauvinism," and thus has been vulnerable to Chinese attack. To make policy decisions affecting the Communist world without recourse to prior consultation or even notification (de-Stalinisation); to apply pressures upon small Communist states or parties to induce conformity (Albania); and to be relatively insensitive to Asian needs, to give assistance in begrudging or penurious fashion—all of these actions and attitudes are noted in Pyongyang as well as in Peking.

Currently, the Chinese loom up in the eyes of "small" Asian Communists as the champions of their right to self-expression and independence—their right to find and develop their own route to Communism with ample external "assistance" but no external "interference." For the moment at least, Communist China is more in tune with the nationalist components of Asian Communism than is the Soviet Union.

At this point, no one can predict where this great struggle within the Communist world will end, or what the ultimate position of North Korea will be. The present trend, however, is clearly towards Peking and away from Moscow in so far as the DPRK government is concerned, and it would be surprising if that trend were to be reversed, at least in the near future.[27] Of course, one cannot foreclose the possibility of rising internal divisions connected with foreign policy stands. Certainly, Khrushchev will not accept a Peking-Pyongyang alliance aimed at him without complaint. And as the North Korean leaders know well, Soviet retaliation can take a number of forms, none of them pleasant. Perhaps the present warnings issued by Premier Kim and others that no true Socialist state could possibly interfere in the internal affairs of another has reference to more than Soviet-Albanian relations.

Meanwhile, with the small members of the Communist bloc, both those in Europe and those in Asia, the DPRK government maintains relations that are outwardly cordial, whatever inner tensions may exist. In early July 1962, for example, the 41st anniversary of the Mongolian revolution was celebrated in Pyongyang with a banquet tendered by the Mongolian Ambassador. Despite the fact that the Mongolian People's Republic remains a staunch Soviet ally—one of the few Communist parties of Asia to support fully the Soviet cause—the speeches made at the banquet suggested complete unity and harmony. Relations with North Vietnam, of course, are much more harmonious in fact, because these two countries share a common outlook and a common set of problems as well as a common geographic position. There is a good deal of evidence that Ho Chi Minh and Kim Il-song have moved toward

[27] Events taking place since this essay was written further confirm this thesis. At the 12th Congress of the Czechoslovakian Communist Party, held December 4–8, 1962, the Korean Workers' Party was openly attacked for the first time by pro-Moscow elements after its spokesman had protested against the continuing criticisms of the Chinese Communists.

At the 6th Congress of the German Socialist Unity Party, January 15–21, 1963, Li Hyo-soon, leader of the KWP delegation, was prevented from delivering his prepared speech orally (although a Tito representative was allowed to speak) and, according to Korean sources, only an abridged version of the speech was released to the delegates in printed form.

Indeed, according to an angry editorial published in the January 30, 1963, issue of *Nodong Sinmun*, the Korean delegation was confronted in East Berlin with open hostility, and the question, "On which side are you?" Chinese Communist organs of this period make it clear that the Chinese regarded North Korea as firmly on their side, along with most other Asian Parties. So did Thorez and other Western Communist leaders. The North Koreans did nothing to deny this assumption. On the contrary, throughout the spring of 1963, *Nodong Sinmun* and other organs of the KWP took positions on all of the burning issues within the bloc virtually identical to those being taken by the Chinese. Pyongyang was now the boldest, most open ally of Peking in Asia.

a true alliance in recent months, seeking to work out both strategies and policies in concert.

NORTH KOREA AND THE " THIRD WORLD "

Towards the vast " non-Western world "—Africa, Asia and Latin America—North Korea has sought to extend her contacts through every conceivable means, confident that the world balance of power can be most easily swung in favour of Communism by concentrating upon these vital regions. Pyongyang is also aware of the fact that the Republic of Korea has shown a greatly increased interest in the non-aligned world. In Latin America, the DPRK government focuses its attention upon Cuba although it invites cultural and political missions from other Latin American states. The ties with Cuba are as intimate as the North Koreans can make them. Cuban students study in Pyongyang; Cuban dance teams perform as a part of cultural exchange; and Cuban leaders visit North Korea, receiving special attention everywhere. Cuba, more than any single country, is a symbol to the North Koreans of the future triumph of Communism over the United States. It is not surprising, therefore, that they greeted the recent Russian retreat with unconcealed dismay.

In Africa, the focus has been upon leftist states of West Africa. During August 1961, a North Korean mission visited the states of Guinea, Mali, Ghana, Morocco and the United Arab Republic by invitation. Subsequently, it was announced that Korea would enter into trade, cultural and postal-broadcast relations with Guinea, trade and cultural relations with Mali, consular relations with the UAR, Morocco and Ghana, and that formal diplomatic relations would be established with Guinea, Mali and Algeria. North Korea, along with other members of the Communist bloc, is thus currently participating in the struggle to determine the political orientation of the last continent to emerge into the universal stream.

For North Korea, Asia remains an area of friends and enemies, a region of promise and threats. Naturally, the DPRK government reacts in a hostile fashion to governments aligned with American power. When this combines with some element of nationalist antagonism, as in the case of Japan, a steady drumfire attack ensues. Since its inception in 1945, the North Korean government has maintained a position of total antagonism to the prevailing Japanese administration. North Korean spokesmen attack Japanese leaders as " Fascists," " militarists " and " reactionaries," who seek to wield nuclear weapons hand in glove with American imperialism. They charge that Japan, aided by the United States, hopes to bring the South Korean " puppets " into their orbit, fostering a NEATO alliance aimed at "the Socialist world." The DPRK government, in company with its auxiliaries in Japan, has done everything possible to sabotage the current talks between Japan and the Republic of Korea.

At the same time, however, the North Koreans have established *de facto* relations with Japan, primarily because of their desire to effect the repatriation of Koreans living in Japan. On August 13, 1958, after a lengthy period of negotiations, the Japanese and Korean Red Cross reached an agreement in Calcutta to repatriate Koreans residing in Japan who wished to return to the North. Up to date, some 80,000 Koreans have been repatriated, with an additional 600,000 remaining in Japan. On November 8, 1962, the agreement was extended without change for another year. This repatriation programme has had both a manpower and a propaganda advantage for North Korea, especially since the Republic of Korea in the south has not offered comparable opportunities. General relations between North Korea and Japan, however, remain minimal, and this is likely to continue as long as the Japanese conservatives continue in power.

Elsewhere in Asia, the North Koreans have rather limited representation, but as noted earlier, they have established consulates in a few of the key neutralist capitals, such as Rangoon, Djakarta and New Delhi, with the hope of expanding from these bases.

CONCLUSIONS

How are we to summarise the foreign policy of North Korea today? In the broadest sense, like the foreign policy of any state, the foreign policy of the DPRK government is a product of geography, historical tradition, and the ideological-political proclivities of the current ruling group. These forces, of course, interact with the larger forces operative in the world around Korea. North Korea is a small country, with a population insufficient even to dominate the Korean peninsula. It is a country, moreover, in Asia and on the peripheries of China. Historically, Korea has always had to contend with the power rivalries of Russia, China and Japan. Today, one can substitute the United States for Japan, and allow the historic problem to stand. Perhaps North Korean foreign policy can be summarised as follows:

1. To maintain the alliances with Communist China and the Soviet Union as a protection against the United States and its allies. (But to count more heavily upon the alliance with China.)

2. To maintain a formal position of non-alignment in the face of the rising Sino-Soviet dispute as long as possible, while exercising maximum pressure to close the breach and, at the same time, siding

with the Peking, hard line policies. To use parlance currently popular in the United States, North Korea belongs to the hawks, not the doves. She supports Peking in an insistence that risks must be taken on behalf of the advancement of Communism, that blows must be struck at the enemy everywhere, that sacrifices must be increased on behalf of National Liberation Movements and the economic-military development of " fraternal Socialist allies." North Korea most certainly does not want to see the Communist bloc broken asunder at this point, but neither is it prepared to abandon these deeply held positions lightly.

3. To pursue a formula for Korean unification closely patterned after that being advanced by the North Vietnamese: an ultimate reliance upon combined political and military tactics. The first step is the creation of a United Front, the development of a political milieu in which Communists can interact with other forces on behalf of nationalist-reformist measures. The second step is the movement into action: the development of a " people's army," the unfolding of guerrilla warfare tactics when the socio-political-economic climate is ripe.

4. To forward the world revolution by concentrating upon the non-Western emergent " third world," exploiting conditions in Africa, Asia and Latin America to weaken and ultimately to topple " imperialism," notably the United States. (Currently, North Korean policy in these respects is, like Chinese policy, uniquely Bolshevik and Leninist *circa* 1920.)

5. To designate the United States World Enemy Number 1, and to oppose any compromise with American policy at present. (North Korea, like the CPR, proclaims a policy of " peaceful coexistence with countries having different social systems." However, this is intended to apply primarily to the " neutralist " world. Towards the United States and its close allies, North Korea follows a policy of vituperation and implacable hostility. Not able to challenge its primary foe militarily and not prepared to settle any of the outstanding issues on terms other than its own, the DPRK government uses all of the techniques of enmity available to it.)

For the present leaders of North Korea, the cold war must continue until their side obtains total victory. Accustomed to a harsh life, they pursue a harsh policy, and like their Chinese comrades, look askance at Soviet " softness." Unless Communist China is removed as a major influence upon North Korea—or unless some internal upheaval replaces the " hawks " with more moderate men, the DPRK government will continue to talk tough even though it must depend mainly upon others to translate this talk into action.

North Korea's Industrial Development During the Post-War Period

By YOON T. KUARK*

SINCE the end of the Second World War, which brought the division of the country into northern and southern halves, North Korea has become a thoroughly orthodox Communist state with but few deviations from the Russian type. The "Marxist-Leninist line" has been followed with fidelity and enthusiasm in the field of economic planning and organisation as laid out in both the early Five-Year Plans of Soviet Russia and in the similar pattern of socialisation in Red China.[1] What deviation exists is said to be characteristic of the transitional period in building Socialism or a "people's democracy," where exploiting elements still exist, as contrasted with the Soviet Union, where it is claimed "Socialism" is a reality. The government so far has launched the two One-Year Plans of 1947 and 1948, the first Two-Year Plan of 1949–50 with emphasis on Soviet assistance, the Three-Year Plan of 1954–56, the first Five-Year Plan of 1957–61, and the Seven-Year Plan of 1961–67.

As a result of the Law of August 10, 1946, more than 1,000 industrial enterprises, comprising 90 per cent. of all the industry of North Korea, were nationalised.[2] Thus, large-scale private factories and enterprises,

* This is an excerpt and updating from the basic research on North and South Korea's Economic Development which was done during the 1960–61 academic year for the Economic Development Workshop Seminar at the University of Minnesota. The author is indebted to Professors M. Bronfenbrenner, J. Schmookler, Anne O. Krueger and fellow members of the Workshop for their valuable comments and suggestions. The author wishes to express thanks to Professor Bronfenbrenner for his help in obtaining microfilm data on North Korea from the U.S. Library of Congress, and also to Mrs. Elizabeth B. Green at the University of Denver for correcting the author's English. Errors and mistakes are the author's own responsibility.

1 Rudolph, Philip, *North Korea's Political and Economic Structure* (New York: Institute of Pacific Relations, 1959), pp. 61–64.

"In overwhelming measure North Korean political and economic institutional development has been patterned on that of the Soviet Union. . . . By utilising Soviet experience, North Korea could repeat much of the Soviet development pattern in a much shorter time. . . . Such differences as exist between the Soviet and North Korean economic institutions are in the realm of theory rather than practice (as in the case of the Soviet collective farm and the North Korean co-operative) . . ." (pp. 61–62).

"North Korea's pattern of socialisation has in many respects resembled that of China rather than that of Eastern Europe, particularly in economic policy since the end of the Korean War. The timing and tempo of collectivisation (although different from the Chinese commune system) closely coincided with that of China . . ." (p. 62).

2 Kim, G. F. "Ekonomicheskoi i Kul'turnoe stroitel'stvo v Koreiskoi Narodno-Demokraticheskoi Respubliki (1945–50 gg.)" ("Economic and Cultural Construction

banks, transportation and communications, the economic foundation of the Japanese exploitation and the " comprador " class were liquidated. Figures reported for 1949, compared with those reported for 1946, show that total industrial output increased 3·4 times and state industry 4·2 times, exceeding the 1944 production level by 20 per cent. The gross output of farm and animal products increased 1·4 times between 1944 and 1949. National income doubled in 1949, as compared with 1946, and factory and office workers' salaries increased 83 per cent. At this juncture the whole country was miserably devastated by the war against South Korea begun on June 25, 1950, on North Korea's initiative.

In the nine years since the fighting stopped, North Korea has become something of a showcase, with plenty of window-dressing and propaganda for Communism in Asia. Great economic strides were claimed for the Three-Year Plan (1954–56) which was fulfilled in two years and eight months.[3] Because of the emphasis on " vast capital construction," the state spent 80,600 million Won[4] in this area, 1,800 million more than originally planned. Out of the total investment during the period of the Three-Year Plan, 73·1 per cent. is said to have been made available for productive construction[5] (58,900 million Won), of which 49·6 per cent. was for industrial construction (39,900 million Won), 9·2 per cent. for agriculture (7,400 million Won), and 13·1 per cent. for transportation and communications (10,600 million Won). The remaining 26·9 per cent. (21,700 million Won) went to the construction

in the Korean People's Democratic Republic, 1945–50 ") *Voprosy Istorii* (1954), pp. 27–42. See also Pak, M. N. *Iz istorii Osvoboditel'nogo dviszheniia Koreiskogo Naroda* (*From the History of the Liberation Movement of the Korean People*) (Moscow: " Zanie," 1955), pp. 46–47.

[3] Bazhenov, G. N. " Koreiskaia Narodno-Demokraticheskaia Respublika no Puti Vosstanovleniia i Razciriia Narodnogo Khoziaistva " (The Korean People's Democratic Republic on the Road to Reconstruction and Development of the People's Economy). *Sovetskoi Vostokovedenie*, No. 2, (1956), pp. 119–127. Also refer to Maslennikov, V. A. (ed.), *Vosstanovlenie i Razcitie Narodnogo Khoziaistva Koreiskoi Narodno-Demokraticheskoi Respubliki* (*Reconstruction and Development of the People's Economy of the Korean People's Democratic Republic*) (Moscow: Izdatel'stvo Inostrannoi Literatory, 1955), p. 186. A study based in part on this source is Shabad, Theodore. " North Korea's Post-war Recovery," *Far Eastern Survey*, Vol. 25 (June 1956), pp. 81–91.

[4] These Won figures are in old Won currency of North Korea. On February 17, 1959, the second currency reform (the former reform, in 1947) was made by which one new Won was exchanged for 100 old Won. *Kyongje Konsol* (Pyongyang) No. 2, February 1959, pp. 2–3. After this currency reform, the exchange rate between the United Kingdom and North Korea was said to be £1 : 7·2 Won. Therefore, the U.S. dollar may be valued at 2·5 Won; Japanese currency at 150 Yen to 1 Won. See *Kita-Chosen no Kiroku* (Records of North Korea) in Japanese (Tokyo: Shindokusho-Sha, 1960), pp. 132–133.

[5] " Productive construction " in North Korea includes: (1) industrial construction, (2) agricultural construction, (3) transportation and communications construction, and (4) construction for commerce and social services; while " non-productive construction " includes: (1) educational and cultural construction, (2) scientific research, (3) housing, and (4) public facilities (like parks, restrooms, museums, etc.). See also *Economic and Statistical Information on North Korea,* JPRS (Joint Publications Research Service) 901-D, Jan. 15, 1960, p. 122.

of educational and cultural establishments. Out of 21,700 million Won, 2,600 million Won (12 per cent.) was spent for dwelling-houses.[6] During the first Five-Year Plan period (1957–61),[7] it was reported that the total value of industrial output had risen more than threefold, and the total value of commodities in circulation about 2·5 times over 1957. It has been claimed that the Five-Year Plan was completed within two and a half years, the rest being called a "transitional period" for the preparation of the second Five-Year Plan, which would start from 1961 instead of 1962 as originally planned.[8] This is now known as the Seven-Year Plan.

It is rather interesting at this point, before going into a morass of detail, to see how the Communist government has financed these projects as a whole. The following tables will be useful for this purpose.

Table 1. Total Capital Formation in North Korea.

(1955 = 100)
(Million old Won)

	In 1950 Prices	In 1955 Prices	Index
1954	24,831	42,213	84·6
1955	29,349	49,893	100·0
1956	26,402	44,883	90·0
1957	27,136	46,131	92·5
1958	34,018	57,831	115·9
Total	141,736	240,951	

[6] *Kyongje Konsol*, November 1957, p. 22, and *Kulloja* (Pyongyang), April 1957, p. 66. The absolute figures in old Won in parentheses are computed by the author from percentage figures and a given total.

However rapidly their plans were accomplished, it is interesting to note that in the speech delivered by Kim Il-song before the Plenum of the Central Committees of the Labour Party in March 1954, "concerning Deficiencies in the Area of Transport and Industry and the Next Tasks of Party, Governmental and Economic Organs in Eliminating these Deficiencies," Kim deplores widespread "bureaucratism," "confusion" and "ignorance."

[7] *Choson Chungang Nyongam 1958*, (*Korean Central Yearbook 1958*) (Pyongyang: Choson Chungang T'ongshinsa, 1958), p. 102–104. Also refer to JPRS, *Economic and Statistical Information on North Korea*, JPRS 901-D, Jan. 15, 1960, pp. 1–2. According to the Resolution on the Concluding Report of the Third Congress of the (North) Korean Labour Party, the Five-Year Plan envisages further promoting Socialist transformation "by speeding Socialist industrialisation and by completing collectivisation of agriculture, to continue the priority development of heavy and light industry; on this basis to ensure rapid progress in all branches of the national economy thereby increasing the material and cultural living standards of our people; and thus to consolidate the source of our revolution into a mighty material base for the peaceful unification and independence of the country."

[8] Akimoto, Hideo, "On the Economy" and "Topics on Heavy Industry," *Kita-Chosen no Kiroku* (*Record of North Korea*) (Tokyo: Shindokusho-Sha, 1960), pp. 75–118. Mr. Akimoto of the Tokyo Yomiuri Shinbun gave an eye-witness account of the "miraculous" story of how the Five-Year Plan was achieved within

Source: *Economic and Statistical Information on North Korea*, JPRS 901–D, Jan. 15, 1960, pp. 221–222, and for 1958 figure, *North Korea's Economic Development Since Liberation* (Japanese Edition) (Pyongyang: Foreign Language Publishing House), pp. 18–19. The figures in 1950 prices were officially published. The 1955 price index was estimated to be 170 when the 1950 price index equalled 100.

Table 2. State Investment for Capital Construction in North Korea

(In million old Won at 1950 prices)

	1954	1955	1956	1957	1958
1. Industry	10,729	15,075	14,144	15,701	18,574
2. Agriculture	1,584	3,092	2,767	1,395	2,619
3. Transport and Communications	4,956	4,631	3,087	1,708	3,619
4. Commerce and Social Services	309	276	399	858	1,157
5. Education and Culture ...	2,055	1,431	1,278	1,259	—
6. Scientific Research	67	145	126	153	1,095
7. Health	329	457	315	430	—
8. Housing	2,625	3,201	3,857	4,060	4,354
9. Public Facilities	1,944	1,540	1,133	1,112	2,041
10. Others	233	571	296	460	408
Total	24,831	29,349	26,402	27,136	34,018

Source: *Economic and Statistical Information on North Korea*, JPRS 901–D, Jan. 15, 1960, p. 222.

In general, the following industrial production indices are interesting and informative in studying North Korea's alleged accomplishments.

Table 3. Indices of Industrial Production in North Korea

(1955 = 100)

	1954	1955	1956	1957	1958
Mining	78	100	132	173	208
Manufacturing	61	100	135	189	212
Electricity	63	100	162	219	235
Overall	67	100	143	194	217

Source: *Economic and Statistical Information on North Korea*, JPRS 901 – D, Jan. 15, 1960, pp. 174–180. The author has recomputed the published data to make 1955 instead of 1953 the base year. See also JPRS *Economic Reports on North Korea* (Nos. 22–25 of series), for 1958 figures.

2½ years. In sum, he cited: (1) " workers' enthusiasm," (2) extensive mobilisation of labour and resources, (3) increase in labour productivity, (4) an effective incentive system, (5) increasing industrial technology, and (6) material and technical aids from the Soviet Union (1,000 million rubles), China (800 million yuan), Czechoslovakia and East Germany (capital equipment), etc., as reasons for this achievement.

Finance

North Korea's budgetary revenue comes mainly from the state and from co-operative enterprises, while tax revenue represents less than one-tenth of the total. Foreign aid received has been gradually decreasing since the record year 1954, with North Korea gradually moving towards being self-supporting. The revenue from Socialist enterprises has steadily increased, reaching 92·5 per cent. of the total in 1958 compared with 53 per cent. in 1954.

Table 4. General State Revenue of North Korea
(Thousand million old Won at current prices)

	1954	1955	1956	1957	1958
Revenue from State	%	%	%	%	%
Co-operative					
Enterprises	47·4(52·9)	74·7(69·1)	74·1(74·7)	102·8(82·2)	112·9(92·5)
Tax Revenue	12·1(13·4)	9·9(9·1)	8·8(8·8)	7·0(5·6)	3·7(3·0)
Foreign Aid	30·7(33·4)	23·5(21·7)	16·4(16·5)	15·3(12·2)	5·5(4·5)
Total Revenue	90·2(100·0)	108·2(100·0)	99·3(100·0)	125·1(100·0)	122·1(100·0)

Source: Karshinov, L. N., *People's Democratic Republic of Korea* (Russian Economic Study) JPRS 15687:3822, Sept. 6, 1960, p. 48 and JPRS 901–D, *op. cit.*, pp. 131–133. The 1958 figures are preliminary.

As for expenditures, the North Korean régime spent annually around 70 per cent. of its budget for its economy (*i.e.*, state investment or capital formation), 15–20 per cent. for social and cultural measures, and the remainder for state administration costs and national defence purposes, which have each run at about 6 per cent. of the total expenditure.

Table 5. State Expenditure of North Korea
(Thousand million old Won at current prices)

	1954	1955	1956	1957	1958
National Economy	%	%	%	%	%
Social and Cultural	63·9(79·3)	84·8(84·4)	83·2(87·0)	89·8(87·8)	100·1(84·4)
National Defence	6·5(8·0)	6·1(6·2)	5·7(5·9)	5·4(5·3)	6·4(5·4)
Administrative Costs	6·8(8·4)	6·4(6·4)	5·9(6·1)	6·2(6·0)	6·6(5·5)
Total Expenditure	80·6(100·0)	100·6(100·0)	95·6(100·0)	102·2(100·0)	118·3(100·0)

Source: Karshinov, *op. cit.*, p. 49 and JPRS 901–D, *op. cit.*, pp. 131–134. Original figures are rounded. The 1958 figures are preliminary. Each item does not add up to the total figure because of miscellaneous items omitted.

Mining and quarrying

Nearly two hundred minerals and ores are known to exist in Korea, but their value lies more in their variety than in the absolute quantity of known deposits. Major mineral resources so far discovered in both North and South Korea include gold, silver, iron, anthracite and bituminous coal, copper, graphite, manganese, molybdenum and tungsten.

During the Three-Year Plan period the North Korean government spent 2,100 million Won to rehabilitate and develop the coal industry—500 million Won in 1954, 700 million Won in 1955 and 900 million Won in 1956. Besides, 1,121 million Won was invested in coal mines in 1957.[9] Sixteen anthracite mines and thirteen bituminous coal mines were restored and expanded, and capacity of coal mining rose considerably. Korea's coal deposits amount to 2,400 million tons, some 70 per cent. of them in North Korea. Coal mining amounted to 3·9 million tons in 1956, which was 5·5 times over 1953, and reached nearly the pre-war level of 1949.[10] Emphasis during the first Five-Year Plan was placed on improving existing facilities and exploiting new mines. Increased anthracite production is planned, and research work is scheduled to be done on ways of converting anthracite into locomotive fuel and gas.

North Korea's two big iron industrial centres are located on the lower reaches of the Taedong River in the vicinity of Pyongyang (North Korea's capital) and in Hamgyong North Province which borders Siberia. Because the ferrous and non-ferrous mines were destroyed by the war, the government is reported to have invested 2,800 million Won to reconstruct them during the Three-Year Plan period. As a result of speedy restoration of the metal industry as of the end of 1956, the capacity of steel increased thirteen times over 1953; that of structural steel increased by 44 per cent. And compared with the end of 1954, the production capacity of electrolytic copper increased by 31 per cent. and electrolytic lead 2·8 times.[11]

In the Three-Year Plan period there was a new production capacity of 100,000 tons of pig-iron. In 1956 the output of steel products, electrolytic copper, lead, silver and crude gold already exceeded the pre-war production level of 1949. Steel production exceeded the 1944 level under the Japanese occupation by 30 per cent., structural steel by 26 per cent., electrolytic copper by 43 per cent., electrolytic lead by 100 per cent., electrolytic silver by 150 per cent. and crude gold by 380 per cent.[12]

The First Five-Year Plan envisioned increases in pig-iron by 2·8-times, iron ingots by three times, steel three to 3·5 times, and steel plate

[9] JPRS 901-D, *op. cit.*, pp. 26–27. These Won figures are in old Won.
[10] JPRS, *Industrial Development in North Korea*. JPRS 566, July 11, 1958, pp. 2–3. See also *Kyongje Konsol*, March 1957, p. 83.
[11] *Kyongje Konsol*, March 1957, pp. 84–86.
[12] *Ibid.*

3·5 to fourfold. More special steel—such as high-speed steel, instrumental carbon steel and various kinds of sheet steel, including silicon sheet steel—is to be produced, while existing mines are to be mechanised and new mines prospected for.

Manufacturing [13]

The North Korean government appropriated 3,100 million Won (in old currency) towards erecting new machine-building factories and restoring the old ones during the Three-Year Plan period. By 1956 machinery production exceeded that of 1949 as follows: lathes, 39 times; electric motors, 13·2 times; winches, 18·5 times; motor vessels, 10 times; pumps, 13·7 times; and farm implements, 16 times. Nevertheless, the machine-building industry is still " the weakest link " and has not caught up with the advance registered by other industries.

The First Five-Year Plan called for mass production of machine-tools, electric appliances, farming and mining machinery, construction machines, engines and vessels. Mining and construction machines such as rock-drills, crushers, winches, compressors, small-sized cranes, turret cranes, mixers, conveyors and excavators will be produced on a mass scale. Taian Electric Appliances Factory—largest of its kind in North Korea—has been further expanded to include a large electric appliances shop. It is reported that a new electric appliances factory in Pyongyang initially turned out electric machines and low-tension appliances; by 1961 it was to produce electric motors, transformers, electric wires and electrometers, and electric appliances for home use. Engineering works, automobile assembly works, and passenger and freight-car repairs shops are built, while small-size ironclad vessels are constructed in some shipyards. The quality of farm implements is being improved, and animal-drawn implements are being replaced gradually with power machines.

Production of chemical fertiliser was emphasised during the Three-Year Plan period and 3,100 million Won earmarked for it, of which 1,720 million Won went for restoring the Hungnam Fertiliser Factory. During the first Five-Year Plan period the Hungnam Fertiliser Factory and the Pongung Chemical Factory were completely rehabilitated. The former already (since 1957) boasts a new nitro-ammonium shop which produces 100,000 tons a year. The annual mineral-fertiliser output is expected to reach 600,000 tons within a few years. Also planned is the production of kalium and other fertilisers, and of insecticides such as DDT, hexafroran and formalin. With the restoration of many damaged chemical factories, annual production capacity showed a marked rise during the Three-Year Plan period: 200,000 tons of ammonium

[13] Summarised from the information given in the series of *Industrial Development in North Korea*, JPRS 408, 566 and 704.

sulphate, 52,800 tons of nitro-lime, 7,500 tons of ammonium chloride, 65,000 tons of ammonia, 146,000 tons of sulphuric acid, 7,000 tons of caustic soda, 7,500 tons of sodium carbonate and 149,000 tons of carbide were produced.

A number of rubber factories, including those at Pyongyang and Sinuiju, were restored and expanded, and the production of belts, hoses and other rubber goods increased. Production facilities for such chemical products as paint and enamel were also restored. Increased production is foreseen for synthetic fabrics made from carbide, alcohol and nitric acid, and for various kinds of medicines. Caustic soda is produced and a large quantity exported. The first up-to-date dye factory in North Korea became operative in Sunchon in 1960.

Scores of factories like the Kangnam and Taesong brickyards, which can produce 150,000 tons of bricks a year, were newly built. By the end of 1956 brick production had increased 2·6 times and roof tiles 6·2 times over 1953, and cement 43 per cent. over 1954, while the annual capacity of sheet-glass production reached 2,400,000 square metres. During the First Five-Year Plan period the output of bricks, roof tiles, artificial slates, natural slates, store products and glass has been increased. Cement production is to reach 2,000,000 tons by 1961, or about three times more than in 1949. The main tasks of capital construction are the improvement of drafting and the wide introduction of the assembly method in building.

During the Three-Year Plan period 7,500 million Won was spent on light industry, 2,200 million of it for the textile industry and 800 million for the food industry. It is reported that thirty light industrial factories were rebuilt or newly established in North Korea. Despite the widespread destruction of factories in the war, textile output in 1956 was said to be three times more than in 1949, and the food-processing industry grew by 127 per cent. It was planned that by the end of the First Five-Year Plan period the annual production of fabrics would reach 17 metres *per capita.* The addition of a rayon shop (using reeds as raw material) in 1957, and the erection of another staple-fibre shop in 1958—both at the Chongjin Mill—mean the production of " tens of millions of metres " of silk and artificial fabrics. (These figures have not been verified, however.) Footwear was turned out at an annual rate of 2·4 pairs *per capita* by 1961. The Sinuiji Enamelled Ironware Factory and the Pyongyang Ceramic Yard were recently built.

Electric power

In 1943 Korea's total electric power generation was 5,688 million kwh., of which South Korea generated only 112 million kwh. Electric power generated in the North was available to the South until May 14, 1948. After that time, South Korea was left with only 198,820 kw. of electric power generating capacity, and consequently faced an acute power shortage, which has since been alleviated to some extent by the installation of 174,000 kw. of new power-generating facilities.

North Korea has the bulk of Korea's hydraulic resources and more than 90 per cent. of the hydro-power generating capability. Of 168 rivers in North Korea more than 4 kilometres long, the longest is the Yalu, which has a potential power of 2,100,000 kwh. Surveys conducted on 64 of the rivers show 200 suitable spots for dams, with a potential capacity of some 8,000,000 kwh., compared with the 1,750,000 kwh. generated as of 1956. Among the large-scale power plants utilising Yalu waters are the Supung (Korea's biggest), with a generating capacity of 700,000 kw., and the following three: Hochungang (338,000 kw.), Changjin (326,000 kw.) and Pujongang (201,000 kw.).

The major objective as regards power during the Three-Year Plan period (5,700 million Won was expended) was the restoration of sixteen big electric-power stations, including the above-mentioned four. Their total electric power-generating capacity reached 1,140,000 kilovolt-amperes, and their annual power generation 5,100 million kwh., an increase of five times over 1953. Transmission and transformer networks, and more than 1,300 kilometres of transmission lines, were also restored, while construction of the Tongnogang Power Station (to generate 90,000 kilovolt-ampere) got under way.

Completion of the First Five-Year Plan in 1961 was expected to bring electricity output to 9,500 million kwh. By then the Tongnogang and Kanggye power plants will have been constructed, and the existing power stations, transmission network, and power-distribution stations rehabilitated and rearranged. Further hydro-electric resources will be explored on the upper reaches of the Taedong, Yalu and Chungchon Rivers.

Workers' wage level

In North Korea it was reported that following the price reduction of 290 items in October 1954, and of 260 items in 1955, an average price cut of 10·3 per cent. was effected by the government on 550 items in 1956. There were seven such price reduction measures enforced by the government. These successive price cuts brought about a general lowering of the price level in state and co-operative trade as well as in private trade.[14] It is also reported that the second currency reform

[14] *North Korea's Economic Development for 15 Years Since Liberation* (Japanese ed.) (Pyongyang: Foreign Language Publishing House, 1960), pp. 38–39. Also see JPRS, *op. cit.*, p. 172. Muraoka, Hiroto, a Japanese newspaperman, reports that

(the first was in December 1947) was completed in February 1959, by which one new Won was exchanged for 100 old Won.[15]

The government ordered several wage increases: 25 per cent. in April 1954, 35 per cent. in November 1956, 10 per cent. in January 1958, and another 40 per cent. in January 1959. As a result, the average real wage level at the end of 1956 was said to have reached the pre-war level of 1949, and the index (using 1949 as the base year) showed 136 in 1957, 159 by 1958.[16] " Since the armistice, workers and office employees have received large sums in social security and social insurance allowance, together with paid vacations in rest-homes and summer camps, free medical treatment and free education. The state implemented a series of measures to increase the supply of rationed food for factory and office workers and their families and to reduce their tax burdens." [17]

Refugees from the North used to report that the take-home pay of North Korean workers after social security, insurance and tax deductions, etc., was so meagre that the workers' " utopia " was actually a hell of disillusionment. However, the seven Japanese journalists who visited North Korea in 1959 reported on their return that the farm, factory, and office workers and their families were leading a " decent " happy life, financially and culturally. The average manager's salary is around 150 Won (in new currency) and the average worker's monthly wage is about 65 Won, while average family expenditures are around 30–35 Won per month.[18] These workers' savings increased 2·2 times in 1957, 4·5 times in 1958, compared with 1956.[19]

Foreign aid

One cannot dismiss the importance of foreign aid in North Korea's industrial development. The economic assistance, both material and technical, which was given by the Soviet Union, Red China and other

" The North Korean Won may be worth about 150 Yen of the Japanese currency, . . . and compared with the Japanese price level, the North Korean prices of daily commodities are unbelievably cheaper while luxury items are far more expensive. . . ." Muraoka, H. " Housing Construction and Citizen's Living," *Kita-Chosen no Kiroku* (*Record of North Korea*), pp. 132–133.

15 JPRS, *Economic Report on North Korea*, JPRS 1700-N, June 18, 1959, pp. 131–132. The North's new Won may be worth 200 Hwan of South Korea as of 1959 when its exchange ratio was $1 : 500 Hwan.

16 *North Korea's Economic Development for 15 Years Since Liberation*, pp. 38–39. See also JPRS, *Economic Report on North Korea* (No. 22 of series) JPRS 2235-N, Jan. 29, 1960, pp. 3–4.

17 *Ibid*. pp. 39–40.

18 *Kita Chosen no Kiroku*, pp. 96–99 and 134–135. Average family size here was three. See also " Housing Construction and Citizen's Life," pp. 121–144, and " Culture, Arts and Sports," pp. 173–191 by H. Muraoka; Narumoto, K., " Education and Welfare Sanitation," pp. 147–169; and Shimizu, I., " Visit to the Farms," pp. 195–211, in the same book.

19 *North Korea's Economic Development*, *op cit*., p. 40.

countries of the Communist bloc, contributed greatly to the reconstruction of the war-shattered economy of North Korea.

Between 1946 and 1949 North Korea received from the Soviet Union a long-term loan of 212 million rubles with an interest rate as low as 1 per cent. per annum. After the end of the Korean War, free aid goods worth 1,000 million rubles were given by the Soviet Union between 1954 and 1956,[20] 800 million Yuan (about 1,320 million rubles at the official exchange rate) by China, 545·4 million rubles by East Germany, 362 million rubles by Poland, 113 million rubles by Czechoslovakia, 25 million rubles by Hungary, 65 million rubles by Rumania, and 20 million rubles by Bulgaria. Albania gave to North Korea free aid in the form of a " great " amount of pitch and crops. Earlier, Mongolia gave 21 carloads of meat, cotton cloth, leather goods and overcoats, and between 1954 and 1956 gave 6,054 head of horses, 39,760 head of sheep, 18,693 head of goats and 446 head of dairy cows.

Since 1956 " a considerable volume of grants and aid goods has been given to North Korea: 300 million rubles by the Soviet Union, 25 million rubles by Rumania, 30 million rubles by Bulgaria, 7·5 million rubles by Hungary, 10,000 tons of pitch by Albania, and 5,000 tons of wheat and 2,000 head of cattle by Mongolia." [21] Besides, North Korea is reported to receive long-term credits from the countries of the Communist bloc as a form of economic co-operation. In October 1960, for example, Peking announced a $105 million loan to North Korea, which will raise China's contribution to around $500 million, versus $750 million from Russia. In November 1960, Moscow announced that the Soviet Union had waived repayment by North Korea of one $190 million Russian loan and had agreed to defer repayment of another $35 million.[22] Taking all this at face value, the total foreign aid received by North Korea amounts to more than 5,000 million rubles, or about 500 rubles *per capita* ($125), during the fifteen years since 1946. Therefore, it may be concluded that both North and South Korea have received about equivalent amounts of foreign aid *per capita* so far, although the effective use of this aid differs considerably.

It was reported that with the aid given by the Soviet Union the Supung Power Plant along the Yalu River, and the Changjin, the Hochon, the Pujon Power Stations, Kimchaik Iron Smeltery, Songjin Steel Works, Manpo Refinery, Hungnam Fertiliser Factory and Madong Cement Factory were rehabilitated and expanded, and the Pyongyang

[20] Karshinov, *op. cit.*, p. 72, confirmed this fact. See also Rudolph, Philip, " North Korea and the Path to Socialism," *Pacific Affairs*, No. 2, June 1959, pp. 133–134. Also see Akimoto, H., " On the Economy," *Kita-Chosen no Kiroku*, p. 85.

[21] JPRS, *Economic Report on North Korea*, JPRS 1291-N, Feb. 26, 1959, p. 78–80. Translated from *Kyongje Konsol*, September 1958, pp. 18–23.

[22] *Time*, Nov. 14, 1960, p. 35.

Textile Mill, Yongsong Meat Packing Plant, Central Broadcasting Station and Red Cross Hospital were rebuilt.[23]

One significant development in 1955 was the liquidation of the joint Soviet-Korean mixed sea-transport and oil-refining companies. It was announced that the Soviet Union would be compensated by deliveries of goods. This step coincided with the cessation of the jointly-owned companies in the other satellite countries.[24]

It was reported that with the aid of China 73 kilometres of railway line were laid and also that three locomotive sheds—Taedong, Chungchon, Daeryong—and iron bridges on the Korea-China frontier were fully restored. A furniture factory and a tile-yard were put into operation with the aid of Bulgaria. The city of Hamhung was reported being rebuilt with the aid of East Germany. A railway factory, and the Aoji, Shinchang and Anju coalmines were rehabilitated with the aid of Poland; a power plant and Haichon Machine Building Plant and an automobile repair shop were built with the aid of Czechoslovakia; a dyeing plant and " new mechanical engineering plant " with the aid of Hungary; a pharmaceutical factory and the Unsan Cement Plant with the aid of Rumania.[25] Besides this, the Soviet Union and the other nations of the Communist bloc rendered a great deal of medical aid by sending doctors, medical supplies and hospital equipment. As for technical aids, these countries sent a number of technicians into North Korean firms and factories. Training of skilled Korean workers in the technical schools, factories and plants of these Communist satellite countries (Eastern Europe) has been carried out intensively.[26] In view of what it has accomplished with foreign aid, the evidence obviously shows that North Korea has done a better job than South Korea in reconstructing its economy.

Conclusions

No judgment can be sound unless all relevant facts are kept in perspective. In the complexities of the North Korean situation, it is quite difficult to assess precisely the entire industrial development without directly verifying the facts in the Communist North. Here caution must be used. Information from North Korea has the following characteristics:

(1) There are no direct means of verifying the information given in official releases which are the only available source of information. The

[23] *Kyongje Konsol*, September 1958, pp. 18–23.
[24] Rudolph, *loc. cit.*, p. 134. See also *New York Times*, May 31, 1955, p. 5.
[25] *Kyongje Konsol*, September 1958, pp. 18–23.
[26] Karshinov, *op. cit.*, p. 59.

official releases tend to mention favourable developments and omit unfavourable ones, aiming at effective propaganda.

(2) The choice of the base year, the frequent change in it, and the use made of percentages instead of absolute figures, make interpretation of the released data difficult.

(3) The concepts used in social accounting and measurement differ from those generally used by South Korea and other Asian countries which have adopted Western practice, which affects their comparability.

(4) There are significant gaps in data, notably: continuous series for money supply; absolute figures for national income; capital formation and industrial output.

But even if one makes allowance for Communist propaganda and window-dressing, however, it appears indisputable to this author that North Korea has made greater economic strides during the post-war period as a whole than has South Korea.

In the industrial sector there is good reason to take at face value the Communist claim that "in 1959 the North produced ten times as much steel as South Korea, and five times more cement,"[27] simply because the accident of geography placed more resources in the North, and the rigorous regimentation of workers would make such a level of production possible. At the present time, however, this is not verifiable.

It is true that North Korea has more industry than South Korea on account of these rich natural resources and electric power, and that the atmosphere of an industrial centre was created during the Japanese occupation, especially during the Second World War. Therefore, whatever North Korea's accomplishments since 1945, they cannot be solely attributed to its Communist régime. It remains to be seen, however, whether the Communists can surpass Japan's *per capita* industrial production in ten years as the ambitious premier, Kim Il-song, prophesied in 1959.

There is no doubt, on the basis of all available evidence, that the North Korean régime has used the foreign aid under its control to restore its war-ravaged economy and develop industry more effectively than the South Korean government. I believe that the injection of this foreign capital into their national income, in accordance with their central planning patterned after the Soviet Union and China, has made their phenomenal industrial progress possible.

In a nutshell, the recent economic offensive of the Communist North,

[27] *Time*, Nov. 14, 1960, p. 35.

with the usual dazzle of unconfirmable statistics,[28] may have a grave impact upon the people of South Korea in their current plight. For there is no better bait to poverty-stricken people than economic advance, and unless the industrial resources of the North are reunited with the agricultural resources of the South, it is difficult to see how the Korean people can survive the enforced division of the nation.

[28] If progress in the North was so significant, the North Korean government might give production figures in absolute terms (as in South Korea) not in percentage increases. North Korean statistics are questionable, even if taken at face value.

Land Reform, Collectivisation and the Peasants in North Korea

By CHONG-SIK LEE

IN a speech delivered at the rally commemorating the fifteenth anniversary of the liberation of Korea, the North Korean Premier announced that the peasants in North Korea were now the owners of large-scale collectivised farms and that they had the firm technical foundation for bumper crops every year without strenuous efforts. He declared: "This is the beginning of a world for our farm villages." Another spokesman of the North Korean régime has stated: "It is easy (or good) to work and enjoyable to live in the co-operativised North Korean farms. There is a bumper crop every year in the constantly changing collectivised fields and the peasants' work and living are literally song and dances." [1]

Careful reading of even the propaganda materials reveals, however, that the millennium is yet to come in North Korea and that the régime has been undergoing a considerable degree of strain in the agricultural sphere. Peasants have been under the severest regimentation and the life of "song and dances" is a remote possibility, if that.

What, then, is the actual condition of North Korean peasants? What transformation have North Korean farms undergone, and how have the changes been accomplished? What is the lot of the peasants on the "co-operativised" farms in North Korea?

When the Russian army marched into North Korea in August 1945 it faced a number of major problems in connection with the task of occupation. One of these was establishing a régime of native personnel sympathetic to Communism, and another was clothing this régime with a semblance of legitimacy and public support.

The first problem was solved with relative ease. The Russian command initially endorsed a popular local leader, Cho Man-sik, as the head of the native governing body over its entire zone of occupation. When the institution of the Five Provinces Administration Bureau

[1] Kim Il-Song, *Choson inmin ui minjokjok myongjol 8.15 haebang 15 chunyon kyongch'uk taehoe eso han pogo.* (A Report Delivered at the Rally Commemorating the Fifteenth Anniversary of the Liberation of August 15 which is the national Holiday of the Korean People) (Pyongyang: Korean Workers' Party Press, 1960), p. 7. Kim Kwang-hyon, in his *Ch'ollima Choson* (*Korea of the Flying Horse*) (Pyongyang: National Press, 1961), p. 61.

gained a degree of legitimacy in North Korea, Cho was replaced by Kim Il-song, the Russian choice for North Korean leadership.

For the second and the more difficult task of winning popular support for the Russian-endorsed régime, such progressive measures as land reform, promulgation of the labour ordinance, which stipulated an eight-hour work day for workers, and the implementation of free and compulsory education were used.

The land reform programme served a particularly important political function for the Russian authorities. In spite of the heavier concentration of industry in North Korea, the Russian zone of occupation was still predominantly agricultural. According to a recent North Korean source, 74·1 per cent. of the North Korean population in 1946 was engaged in agriculture.[2] But the majority of the peasants had little or no land of their own. According to Kim Il-song's report of 1947, 6·8 per cent. of the farmers held 54 per cent. of the tilled land in North Korea, while 56·7 per cent. were classified as " poor farmers " and held only 5·4 per cent. of the land.[3] Except for approximately twenty per cent., who were self-employed, the North Korean farmers belonged either to the " pure " tenant-farmer category and had no land of their own or to the " poor farmer " category and worked their own small plots along with the land held by wealthier landlords.

This lopsided distribution of land, coupled with an iniquitous system of farm rent (farm rent averaged from 50 per cent. to 60 per cent. of the crops, often mounting to 70 per cent.) had caused much unrest among the peasants under Japanese rule. Many peasants were forced to abandon their farms and tenancies to migrate to Manchuria. Strikes of tenant farmers had been frequent throughout Korea, even though the Japanese government discouraged them. For these reasons, Communist agitation and propaganda among the peasants during the 1930s, particularly in the more mountainous Hamgyong Pukto, was very effective.[4] Although the situation in the other provinces in North Korea was considerably better than that in Hamgyong Pukto, grievances did exist among the poorer elements of the agricultural population, and the Communist-led " peasants union " movement had a fairly strong following. It is not surprising, therefore, to find that the Russian

[2] *Facts about Korea* (Pyongyang: Foreign Languages Publishing House, 1961), p. 9.

[3] Kim Il-song, " What Should the Parties and Social Groups Demand on the Occasion of the Establishment of the Democratic People's Republic of Korea," dated June 14, 1947, in *Kin Nichisei Senshu* (*Selected Works of Kim Il-song*), (Kyoto: Sanichi Shobo, 1952), I, p. 217. In his speech of April 20, 1948, Kim revised the statistics to 6·8 per cent. of the landlords holding 58·8 per cent. of land: *ibid*. Supp. Vol., p. 114.

[4] See Thought Section, Prosecutor's Bureau, High Court, *Shiso iho* (*Ideological Report Series*), No. 11, (June 1937), pp. 146–170.

authorities in North Korea assigned priority to winning the support of the peasants and that the land reform programme was employed for this task.

On February 8, 1946, the North Korean Interim People's Committee was established in Pyongyang after a conference of the "political parties, social organisations and local people's committees." This conference also decided upon the "impending duties" of the new Interim People's Committee, which, of course, included the land reform programme. The second of the eleven articles stated: "Preparations [will] be made to dispose of, within a short period, the land and forests confiscated from the Japanese aggressors and pro-Japanese reactionary elements. Land and forests subject to confiscation from Korean landlords will be nationalised, the land-tenant system will be abolished, and the land will be distributed to the peasants without compensation."[5] On March 5, the committee, ostensibly adopting the proposals of the Peasants Federation which had demanded the agricultural reform, proclaimed the ordinance on land reform.[6]

The ordinance stipulated that all land formerly possessed by Japanese imperialists (including the government, civilians and organisations), national traitors, Korean landlords with more than five *chongbo* (a *chongbo* is 2·45 acres), absentee landlords, and churches, monasteries and other religious organisations with more than five *chongbo*, and all land continuously held in tenancy, be confiscated without compensation and be distributed without charge to landless peasants or peasants with little land. The ordinance further stipulated that all debts owed by peasants to landlords would be voided and that all farm animals, farm machinery, and houses formerly owned by landlords should be confiscated and then distributed among the peasants. The government, however, retained the option of transferring all the buildings to schools, hospitals, and other social groups. Further, the peasants were prohibited from selling, renting, or mortgaging their newly acquired land. Irrigation facilities formely owned by expropriated landlords and all forests, except small forests owned by peasants, were confiscated and transferred to state ownership.[7]

5 "Political and Organisational Policies of the Workers' Party," Dec. 25, 1947, *Kin Nichisei Senshu*, I, pp. 264–265.

6 Kwahakwon Yoksa Yonguso (Academy of Science, Centre for Historical Studies), *Choson t'ongsa* (*Outline History of Korea*) (Pyongyang: Academy of Science Press, 1958) [Hak-u Sobang reprint edition, Tokyo, 1959], III, p. 31.

7 *Ibid.* p. 32. For an English text of the land reform ordinance see *Report of the United Nations Commission for the Unification and Rehabilitation of Korea* (New York: United Nations, General Assembly, Official Records: Sixth Session, Supplement No. 12 (A/1881), 1951), pp. 59–60.

Table I. Origins of the Confiscated Land, 1946

Owners	Area (*chongbo*)
Japanese Government, nationals and organisations ...	100,797
National traitors	21,718
Landlords with more than five *chongbo*	285,692
Landlords who rent all of their land	338,067
Landlords who continuously rent their land	239,650
Churches, monasteries and other religious groups	14,401
Total	1,000,325

Source: *Kin Nichisei Senshu*, Supp. Vol., p. 115; also in *Choson T'ongsa*, III, p. 34, quoted from *Choson Chungang Nyongam* (*Korean Central Almanac*), 1949, pp. 71–72.

Table II. Disposition of the Confiscated Land, 1946

Recipients	Number of families	Area (*chongbo*)
Farm labourers	17,137	22,387
Tenants without land	442,973	603,407
Farmers with little land	260,501	345,974
Landlords wishing to farm in new localities ...	3,911	9,622
Total	724,522	981,390

Source: *Kin Nichisei Senshu*, Supp. Vol., p. 115; also in *Choson T'ongsa*, III, pp. 34–35.

How was it that the peasants with admittedly retarded class consciousness were " aroused " in such a short period to make the land reform successful? What were the actual functions of the cadres dispatched from Pyongyang and the provincial headquarters of the Party? How was the resistance of the landlords overcome? The tactics employed in executing the land reform deserve to be elaborated beyond the bare outlines and the statistics provided by Communist sources. The North Korean experience deserves scrutiny particularly because, unlike that of neighbouring China, it was accompanied by little bloodshed.

A prize-winning novelist in South Korea, Hwang Sun-won, depicts the entire process of land reform masterfully in fictionalised form in his novel *K'ain Ui Huye* (*The Heirs of Cain*). Hwang, a North Korean, escaped to the south in May 1946, and evidently had first-hand knowledge.

The cadres dispatched from Pyongyang, according to Hwang, were mindful to execute the land reform with the least disturbance and resistance. The programme was to be carried out in the name of the peasants and, therefore, it required their direct participation. The cadres began by nurturing an atmosphere conducive to smooth functioning. Their first course of action was effectively to ostracise the landlords and to isolate them from the other peasants. Mere intimation that it would not be to their own advantage to associate closely with their former landlords was sufficient to make most of the tenant-farmers shun the landlords, who in many cases had developed friendly relationships with their tenants. The landlords were then constantly harassed by frequent questioning by the cadres and the police and were placed under close observation. Local tenant-farmers, particularly those with a record of close collaboration with the landlords, such as former tenant-foremen, were chosen as heads of the peasants' committees to aid the cadres. This system provided those with dubious records an opportunity to rectify their past mistakes; the chosen ones, who had the best knowledge of the community, showed enthusiasm and ruthlessness in their new duties, not realising that they would also be purged at a later date.

The peasants were at first sceptical of the land reform ordinance. They would not believe that the land could be distributed without compensation to the owner. They were excited by the possibility that the land could be theirs, but they were embarrassed by their own excitement: How could one take the property of someone else without compensation? Would it not amount to robbery? The peasants were not easily convinced by the cadres' argument that the land originally belonged to them. Many of the peasant families had never owned a plot of land for generations.

The peasants' curiosity, however, was aroused. Landlords seemed to be powerless before the new government. It was obvious to all that the land would be taken away from the former owners, regardless of the local peasants' attitudes. Should one resist the temptation of free land, resist the government in power and, indeed, resist what appeared to be the current of the time? But, if so, why? Was it not clear that the landlords were doomed, regardless of one's efforts? Under these circumstances, would it not be prudent to follow the cadres' instructions more willingly, thereby perhaps obtaining a better piece of land? The peasants' consciences were clear; they did not initiate the land reform programme, and, in fact, they loathed it. They were as helpless as the landlords.

When the first part of the actual land reform was begun—that is, the confiscation of landlords' properties—the cadres were careful not to involve any large number of landlords on any one occasion. Undue agitation of landlords as a class should be avoided, lest they should organise themselves for revolt. Confiscations of land would take place sporadically; confiscations would not even take place simultaneously within a prefecture. Only the properties of the absentee landlords and the large landowners would be confiscated at first. Another round would reach the lower level. This scheduling left landlords with smaller properties a faint hope that they might be spared. It assured the régime of minimal resistance at each stage and even some co-operation from those spared at a particular stage. Human greed and instinct for survival seem to know no bound; and when the price for survival was mere acqiescence in others' destruction, the price was willingly paid.

There was no recourse for the purged landlords. They could gain freedom only by fleeing from Communist jurisdiction and escaping south of the 38th Parallel. In North Korea they would either be arrested and sentenced to an indefinite period of hard labour, transferred to another locality with a small plot of land, or maltreated by the new local authorities and simply chased away. Crossing the "border" at the 38th Parallel became more and more difficult as time went by. There was no time to be wasted. Many purged and yet-to-be purged landlords chose South Korea as their future home.[8]

Being assured of the success of the land reform programme, the authorities in Pyongyang immediately moved towards further consolidation of its bases. This phase of the programme entailed two areas of activity: organisation and discipline of the peasants, and the increase of food production.

Organisation of the peasants had, in fact, been begun even before land reform was put into effect. Domestic-faction Communists had appealed to those of the "poor peasants" class immediately after the Japanese surrender on August 15, 1945, and carried on a broad campaign to enlist them in the Communist Party. We do not know how many peasants were inducted at various stages of the campaign, but, according to Kim Il-song, more than 105,000 members of the North Korean Workers' (Communist) Party in July 1946, were of "poor peasant" origin.[9] Efforts to enlarge the membership of the Party continued, and by March 1948, Kim reported the total to be more than 700,000 members, of which 374,000 were of "poor peasant" origin. It is significant that while the total rose by 90·3 per cent. during the

[8] The estimated number of refugees in South Korea of North Korean origin on Dec. 31, 1947, was 1,116,600. *First Part of the Report of the United Nations Temporary Commission on Korea* (New York: General Assembly, Official Records: Third Session, Supplement No. 9 (A/575), 1948), I, p. 23.

[9] *Kin Nichisei Senshu,* III, p. 48. The party members of worker (proletariat) origin at this time were 73,000 and the total membership was 366,000. *Ibid.* p. 47.

twenty months, the membership of "poor peasant" origin showed more than a threefold increase.

The Party was not the only organ used to organise the peasants. Peasants' federations, the Democratic Youth League and the Women's League carried out equally vigorous campaigns for membership. Membership of an individual in the Party or any one of the organisations did not make him ineligible for membership in another group. The intensity of the membership campaign is indicated by the following two sets of figures presented by Kim Il-song [10]:

	April 1946	July 1946
Peasants' federations	800,000	1,800,000
Workers' Leagues	350,000	350,000
Democratic Youth League ...	500,000	1,000,000
Women's League	350,000	600,000
Total	2,000,000	3,750,000

It is important to note that the membership of the workers' leagues did not increase at all during the three-month period, while that of the peasants' federations more than doubled. The rise in the membership of the other two organisations also doubled or nearly doubled. It is reasonable to assume that most of the new members of the young persons' and women's organisations were from the rural areas.

The Pyongyang government immediately began to utilise the peasants' organisations for the purpose of solving economic problems. Kim Il-song declared on February 19, 1947, that "the immediate task of the North Korean agricultural economy is the solution of the food problem. North Korea must be transformed from a region of food shortage into a region of abundance. This can be done by enlarging the area of cultivation and increasing the rate of production." [11] Kim specified further that in 1947 the area of cultivation would be increased by 300,172 *chongbo* (735,421 acres), an increase of 15·5 per cent. as compared to 1946, and that 155,000,000 Won would be invested by the People's Committee in the expansion of irrigation facilities. The use of chemical fertilisers would also be accelerated, from 109,000 tons in 1946 to 187,000 tons in 1947.

Implicitly, the peasants in North Korea were warned to brace themselves for a period of hard labour. Kim Il-song's speech of April 13,

[10] The figures for April are from his speech on land reform, Apr. 13, 1946, at the first enlarged committee meeting of the North Korean Provisional People's Committee. *Kin Nichisei Senshu*, I, p. 18. The figures for July are from his report on the establishment of Democratic People's United Front, July 22, 1946. *Ibid.* p. 64.

[11] A report on the People's Economic Development Plan for 1947, at the conference of North Korean provincial, municipal and prefectural People's Committees. *Kin Nichisei Senshu*, I, p. 180.

1946, summing up the results of the land reform programme, included the following paragraph:

> The peasants must help each other and mobilise all labour power for the sake of the [successful completion of the] first movement to increase agricultural production since the liberation. The economic and financial foundations of Korea are still weak. Therefore, it is important for us to mobilise labour power fully. We must organise "Build the Nation" labour-service corps and systematically organise and guide the construction and repair of the irrigation facilities. . . .[12]

Later Kim reported that the peasants had shown creativity in developing irrigation works on a broad scale, completing 58 irrigation projects in 1947 alone, for irrigating 19,753 *chongbo* of ricefields.[13] In January 1950, Kim made it known that the irrigation works at Anju must be completed. "For this purpose," he declared, "the entire people and all civil engineers must be mobilised." [14]

In spite of these duties required of the peasants, they were promised a prosperous life. The ordinance on tax in kind for farm products, proclaimed June 27, 1946, specified that the peasants would be "exempt from all taxes on land and rent," and would submit instead only 25 per cent. of their total harvests (rice, other grains, beans and potatoes), being permitted to dispose of the surplus at free markets. On May 1, 1947, the ordinance was amended so that the tax in kind would be 27 per cent. on paddy land, 23 per cent. on dry land and only 10 per cent. on "fire field." [15] Compared to the 50 to 60 per cent. of the crops that tenants paid to their landlords before the land reform, this was indeed a significant improvement.

The peasants, however, were not permitted to enjoy their improved economic status for long. Ambitious economic development plans instituted by the Pyongyang government demanded more than token co-operation from the peasants. The economic plan for 1947, the first of the development plans to be instituted in North Korea, called for a rapid reconstruction of industries to double the production of 1946. The workers were called to increase their productivity by 48 per cent. An increase in coal production and an improvement in transportation facilities were also demanded.[16] Should not the peasants be permitted to participate in the movement for progress?

[12] *Ibid.* p. 16.

[13] *Ibid.* Supp. Vol., p. 116, speech of Apr. 20, 1948.

[14] *Ibid.* p. 198, speech of Jan. 25, 1950.

[15] For the text of the ordinance see *Report of the United Nations Commission for the Unification and Rehabilitation of Korea*, 1951, p. 60. See also U.S. Department of State, *North Korea: A Case Study in the Techniques of Takeover*, p. 57. "Fire field" indicates the areas cleared for cultivation by fire but abandoned in a few years when fertility of soil was exhausted.

[16] For Kim Il-song's report on the economic development plan of 1947 see *Kin Nichisei Senshu*, I, pp. 170–183. Kim noted in this connection that the number of

Already, in 1947, Kim Il-song had announced publicly that an extensive movement for the donation of "patriotic rice" had been started among the farmers by Kim Che-won and was making a great contribution towards national development. This "manifestation of passionate patriotism by the North Korean peasants," Kim said, had brought in such large donations of rice that there was "more than enough for the construction of the fatherland." He declared that the government intended to use the 1,500 ton surplus of rice in 1947 towards the building of a large-scale modern university in Pyongyang.[17] We can assume that the amount of "patriotic rice" donations would be expected to increase as the "peasants' patriotism" was intensified during the successive years. Official sources revealed that the peasants began to donate "large sums in foodstuffs and money" to enable the government to purchase military aircraft.[18] The peasants, along with the rest of the society, were required to purchase assessed amounts of the public bonds which the government began to issue in large quantities in late 1949. As the Korean War drew near and the Pyongyang régime mobilised all available resources in preparation for war, the material benefits that had accrued to the peasants by the land reform programme were reduced to virtually nil.

The opening of the war in 1950 brought about a major disruption in North Korean agriculture, as in every other sector of the economy. Many villages that lay in the path of war were destroyed. Many peasants, young and old, were conscripted for army service before and during the war, and the casualty rate during the war was very high. Furthermore, a great number of North Korean peasants abandoned their farms during the short period of the United Nations occupation of North Korea and moved to South Korea. In short, the socio-political and economic fabric of North Korean agriculture was broken down almost completely.

If the war meant economic disaster for North Korea, however, it at least provided the leaders with an opportunity to review their past performance and plan for future development. We have no means to determine the exact thoughts of the North Korean leadership, but Kim Il-song's speech of December 21, 1950, at the third congress of the central committee of the Communist Party rings with bitterness against

workers, engineers, technicians and office clerks must be increased by 156,000 or 20 per cent. in 1947, as compared to 1946. This additional labour force was to be drawn from the farms.

[17] *Ibid.* p. 246.

[18] *Cho Chung ch'inson nongop hyoptong chohap nongmin dul ui munhwa wa p'ungsup* (*Culture and Customs of the Peasants in the Korea-China Friendship Agricultural Co-operative*) (Pyongyang: Academy of Science Press, 1960), Folklore Research Series, No. 4, p. 211. For a discussion of the inflated assessment of the crop for tax purposes and the quality of crop required for tax, etc., see U.S. Department of State, *op. cit.*, pp. 57–59.

poor performance and weak discipline among the Party cadres. Nor was the Premier satisfied with the cadres' achievements among the masses. Despite the rapid increase of membership in the Party and the auxiliary organisations, the Party had not been able to muster the support it needed from the people during the most trying period of its existence.

Indeed, the weakness of the Party's educational activities was manifested everywhere. By the Premier's own admission, some North Koreans co-operated with the enemy. " Some joined the local security units [formed against the Communists by the Republic of Korea authorities], anti-Communist groups, and other reactionary groups to murder, insult, and suppress the members of the Workers' Party and its supporters." [19]

There are reasons to believe that the Party decided to rectify these weaknesses, particularly the paucity of propagnada and " political education " directed towards the masses, by changing the economic structure in North Korea. The land reform may have eliminated the " feudalistic components " of society, but this was far from creating necessary conditions for the transition to the Socialist stage of economy.

It was only natural that the peasants would retain and even develop " capitalistic thought " under the system of private ownership of land. When the " poor peasants " were allotted pieces of land, their appetite for land and material goods was heightened to a new degree and their pecuniary interest was sharpened more than ever. Instead of arousing the revolutionary consciousness which the Communist leaders seem to have hoped for, the peasants under the new system tended to develop political complacency. The Communist theoreticians should have realised that the land reform merely eliminated the contradiction between the means of production and the productive forces that had existed before and did not create the conditions necessary for the growth of " workers' consciousness " or " revolutionary consciousness."

Thus the land reform in fact dichotomised the society into two distinct sectors: the socialised urban sector of the proletariat and the more capitalistic rural sector. Only by depriving the peasants of their private ownership of the means of production could the Party be assured that the gap would be filled and workers' consciousness developed among the peasants.[20] Stalin's " law of development " also required the subordination of agriculture to the direction of Socialist industry.

[19] *Kin Nichisei Senshu*, II, p. 141.

[20] The North Korean Communists were hard put to justify the collectivisation programme. Thus a North Korean theoretician, Cho Chae-son, was forced to admit that " The Socialistic transformation of the agriculture is a *special* (or *unusual*) *application* of the law of (interrelationship between) the characteristics of productive

While these ideological and political considerations were compelling North Korean leaders to re-examine the régime's agrarian policies, economic conditions in North Korea after the war seem to have compelled them to take immediate action. Grain output decreased during the war [21] and the food shortage was severe. North Korea found it necessary to import at least 5 to 10 per cent. of its consumption needs not only during the war, but for several years afterward. Even in 1961, when the North Korean radio was jubilantly announcing bumper crops in the collectivised fields, the régime found it necessary to import 45,000 metric tons of grain from Australia.[22]

In addition to these problems there was an acute labour shortage. The North Korean loss of population during the war, including migration to the south and war casualties, was estimated to be about 2·1 million persons.[23] Industrial development required the mobilisation of labourers from rural areas. According to official statistics, the proportion of peasants in the population declined from 74·1 per cent. in 1946 to 66·4 per cent. in 1953 and to 44·4 per cent. in 1960. In other words there was a shift of approximately 20 per cent., or 200,000 persons from rural areas to the urban centres between 1953 and 1960.[24] Serious

forces and the productive relations during the transitional period toward Socialism." (Italics added.) In his explanation of this "special application" of the Marxist law, Cho cited the "positive reaction of the new superstructure," *i.e.*, the dictatorship of the proletariat, and the harmful effect of the imbalance between the Socialist industrial sector and the privately managed agriculture. He added further that the imbalance has been noticeable at the latter part of the two-year People's Economic Plan (1949–50). Cho Chae-son, *Choson Minjujuui Inmin Konghwaguk Sahoe Kyongje Chedo* (*The Socio-Economic System in the Democratic People's Republic of Korea*) (Pyongyang: Korean Workers' Party Press, 1958), pp. 38–39.

21 According to a North Korean source, the sown area and grain output decreased as follows:

	1948	1951	1952	1953
Sown area	100	89·2	95·6	97·4
Grain output	100	84·9	91·9	87·2

Data from *Agricultural Co-operativisation in D.P.R.K.* (Pyongyang: Foreign Languages Publishing House, 1958), p 8.

22 U.S. Department of State, Bureau of Intelligence and Research, "Research Memorandum," June 21, 1962, RSB-105, p. 13. (Processed.)

23 *Ibid.* p. 14.

24 The percentages by occupation divisions of and total population of North Korea are reported to be as follows:

	1946	1949	1953	1956	1960
Workers and office employees	18·7%	26·0%	29·7%	40·9%	52·0%
Farmers	74·1	69·3	66·4	56·6	44·0
Others	5·0	2·9	2·4	2·0	3·3
Total	100·0%	100·0%	100·0%	100·0%	100·0%
Population (thousands)	9,257	9,022	8,491	9,359	10,789

Facts About Korea (Pyongyang: Foreign Languages Publishing House, 1961), p. 9. The population figures were taken from U.S. State Department, "Research Memorandum," p. 14.

as the agrarian problems were, industrial development took priority over agriculture.

It is against this background that the " co-operativisation " movement was initiated. After a brief " experimental stage " between August 1953 and October 1954, the Pyongyang régime decided to launch a full-scale collectivisation movement at the Communist Party's central committee's plenum in early November 1954.[25] Within the first year—by December 1955—49 per cent. of the peasants were collectivised. Another 30 per cent. were collectivised during the following year. By December 1957, three years after the co-operative movement had been initiated, 95·6 per cent. of the peasants were organised into 16,032 co-operatives with an average of 64 households each. By August 1958, the entire farm population in North Korea had been inducted into co-operatives and minor adjustments of the size of co-operatives had been made; there were then 13,309 co-operatives with an average of 80 households each.[26]

In October, only two months after the announcement of the " victorious completion of the agricultural co-operativisation movement," the régime proclaimed that the co-operatives would be reorganised into larger units. Henceforth, the *ri*—originally the lowest administrative unit, roughly equivalent to a precinct, but enlarged by the North Korean régime to encompass several villages—would serve as the unit for co-operatives. Instead of 13,309 co-operatives there would be only 3,843 and each would consist of an average of 300 households rather than 80. The average acreage of a co-operative would be 500 *chongbo* (1,225 acres) rather than 130 *chongbo*.[27]

There is little room for doubt that the sudden reversal of the previous policy was brought about by the North Korean leaders' fascination with and idealisation of the commune movement in China. It is to be noted that the Chinese Communists began the merger of co-operatives in April 1958, and in August the Politburo of the Chinese Communist Party ordered the adoption of the commune system throughout China. The enthusiasm of the Chinese Communists was promptly echoed by North Koreans.[28]

[25] Pak Mun-gyu, the Minister of Agriculture from September 1948 to March 1954, was replaced by Kim Il-song's comrade of the partisan days, Kim Il, in March 1954. Kim Il served as Vice-Premier and Minister of Agriculture until September 1957. Kim Il became First Vice-Premier in 1959. Pak Mun-gyu, an agrarian economist of long standing, was relegated to a less important cabinet post.

[26] For a detailed treatment of the process of collectivisation see my article, " The ' Socialist Revolution ' in the North Korean countryside," *Asian Survey*, II, No. 8 (Oct. 1962), pp. 9–22.

[27] *Kim Il-song Sonjip* (*Selected Works of Kim Il-song*) (Pyongyang: Korean Workers' Party Press, 1960), VI, p. 185

[28] See " Chungguk eso ui sahoejuui konsol ui taeyakchin " (" The Great Leap Forward in the Socialist Construction in China "), *Kulloja* (*The Worker*), No. 155, Oct. 15, 1958, p. 77.

Just as in the Chinese communes, the organ of the government, *ri*, was merged with the organisation in charge of production, the co-operative. The co-operative become at once a basic social unit and a basic organisation of state power in that it is designed to integrate rural industry, agriculture, trade, culture and education, and military affairs into a single whole.

Even official North Korean sources admitted that the bulldozing of the collectivisation programme had been accompanied by outright coercion and intimidation along with propaganda. " In some places," according to a North Korean booklet,

> organisational work was undertaken in a bureaucratic manner or as a campaign, on the pretext of overtaking and surpassing those areas where the co-operative movement had advanced faster. In so doing, the degree of preparedness of the peasants was not taken into consideration and various unfair methods were used in drawing some irresolute peasants into co-operatives. . . . Such deviations were also to be seen in the practice of showing contempt for individual farmers and encroaching upon their interests under the pretext of consolidating and developing co-operatives.[29]

Resistance of the farmers to the radical collectivisation programme was by no means negligible. Although no violent uprisings were reported by North Korean sources, cases of evasion and sabotage were not infrequent. Premier Kim summed up the situation in a speech delivered before a conference of the leaders of the co-operatives in 1959 in pointed language:

> Class enemies slandered our Party's policies and spread reactionary rumours opposing the agricultural co-operativisation movement. They also fought to destroy our agricultural co-operatives by damaging common properties or obstructing production. Especially when agricultural co-operativisation was near completion and Socialist victory was becoming more consolidated in cities and farms, the anti-revolutionary elements' infiltration, destruction, and obstructive behaviour became more vicious.[30]

North Korean authorities also encountered considerable difficulty in executing the collectivisation programme because of the lack of well-trained cadres. Violation of democratic management principles, inadequate planning, poor utilisation of co-operatives' properties and financial mistakes were cited as some of the mistakes committed by the " executives." An official source also reported that

> among the managerial personnel of some co-operatives were found subversive elements who had crept into the co-operatives and managed to occupy the leading positions. The defects of officials not only led to

[29] *Agricultural Cooperativization in D.P.R.K.*, pp. 37–38.
[30] *Kim Il-song Sonjip*, VI, p. 175.

waste of labour but also a drop in the rate of co-op members' attendance at work, causing a hindrance to important farm work.[31]

Collectivised farms in North Korea are still called co-operatives, but in fact they differ only very slightly from the artel type *kolkhozy* (collective farms) in the Soviet Union and the communes in China. All land formerly held by individual farmers is now controlled by co-operatives which theoretically own the land. Individual farmers, who work as members of " work teams " or " brigades," under the co-operatives, are paid in kind and cash at the end of the year according to the work days contributed. Farmers are allowed to own a private garden plot, fruit trees, cattle and bees, although data on the extent of these possessions are not available.

In theory, each co-operative is an independent entity and the farmer has full authority to control the affairs of his co-operative through either the co-operative general assembly or the representative assembly which elect the chairman and the members of the co-operative committees. In practice, however, the co-operatives form an integral part of the national economy, and each co-operative is rigidly controlled by the " management committees " at the *kun* (prefectural) level which were created by the Party's central committee plenum in November-December, 1961. It should be noted that the central committee of the Workers' Party admitted, at the time of the establishment of the management committees, the inadequacy of the co-operative officials in meeting the demand for increased production and the deficiency of the " administrative (or bureaucratic) method " used by prefectural people's committees in guiding the co-operatives. The prefectural people's committees still exist as administrative agencies of government but they are deprived of power over agricultural production and management. The new management committees are staffed by agro-technicians from central government organs.[32]

Under the " co-operative system," the state exercises rigid control over the farmers' income and consumption. Since grain dealers were eliminated by decree in October, 1954, and the state-operated stores constitute the only channel for farmers' disposal of their surplus products, state control and supervision is easily facilitated. The régime has instituted a progressive scale of tax in kind, compulsory purchase of farm products with price differentials, and compulsory accumulation of funds and grains at the co-operative level. Although the official figure for tax in kind was reduced from an average of 20·1 per cent. between 1956 to 1958 to 8·4 per cent. after 1959, actual rates of tax collection

[31] *Agricultural Cooperativization in D.P.R.K.*, p. 43.
[32] *Cf. Nodong Shinmun*, Dec. 25, 1961, editorial.

and compulsory savings at the co-operative level cannot be accurately determined.

The life of co-operative peasants is regimented, disciplined and organised to the minute. The demands heaped upon peasants seem to have no limit.

A Japanese reporter sympathetic to the North Korean régime describes the daily schedule of the North Korean farmers as it was related to him by the head of a co-operative:

> [Members of the co-operative] gather on the farm (or in the workshops) around 8.30 in the morning at the signal of a bell from the co-operative. Each member receives instructions from his group leader regarding the day's work. At noon, the bell will ring again and members can go either to the public dining hall or their own homes for lunch. There are circle meetings for drama, music and dancing during the lunch hour. Peasants rest ten to twenty minutes after fifty minutes of work. During the breaks, there are " news reading meetings " when newspapers or magazines will be read aloud. After a day's work, members have their work evaluated and they receive certain points which are recorded in their Labour Notebook. Distribution of crops or cash at the end of the year is done according to the total points accumulated. . . . After work, members with their Labour Notebooks either return home or go to a common bathhouse. They see movies, listen to the radio, or join circle activities.[33]

Even this idealised version does reveal the extent to which the peasants are regimented. In terms of daily work, the above story omits a vital part, *i.e.*, the " voluntary " work undertaken by the peasants. In December 1959, for instance, the Democratic Youth League in the co-operative visited by the Japanese reporters is supposed to have decided to collect three tons of " mud coal " a month per person. The " mud coal " was to be used either as fuel or fertiliser.[34] Earlier in 1958, when the régime had decided to execute a " people's movement for light industry," a variety of " factories " had been established at co-operatives to produce consumers' products.[35] The labour required for irrigation works, construction of schools, roads and houses had to be furnished by the peasants on a " voluntary," hence unpaid, basis.

The régime has evidently decided that overwork and the lack of material incentives can be offset by further indoctrination and intimidation of the peasants. For instance, in the " Korea-China Friendship Agricultural Co-operative," which consisted of 750 families with 1,227 co-operative members as of December 1959, there were fifteen party-policy study groups with some 600 members " guided " by fifty-nine

[33] Ho-Cho Kishadan (Reporters' Group Visiting Korea), *Kita-Chosen no Kiroku (Record of North Korea)* (Tokyo: Shin Dokusho-sha, 1960), pp. 200–201.
[34] *Ibid.* p. 206.
[35] Tera Goro, *38 Dosen no Kita (North of the 38th Parallel)* (Tokyo: Shin Nippon Shuppansha, 1959), p. 106.

agitators and seven " conversation leaders." The co-operative maintained six " Korean Workers' Party History Study Rooms " along with sundry kinds of circles and " mass political edification networks." [36] The function of the " agitators " and " conversation leaders " is to visit the working teams during their rest periods and " explain " the Party's policy and the domestic and international developments. The co-operative, which is one of the " model co-operatives " in North Korea, has also been favoured by the frequent visits of " concentrated guidance groups " dispatched by the central committee of the Party.[37] In order to guarantee the effect of the Party's activities in the co-operatives, the Party interspersed indoctrination activities with occasional " struggles against the counter-revolutionary elements " in the co-operatives, which exposed " liquidated landlords, collaborators with the enemy during the temporary retreat period, and Christian ministers and elders." Some of the purged are alleged to have attempted to collaborate with espionage agents dispatched by the enemy.[38] These purges (the report on the " Korea-China " co-operative mentions purges in 1957 and 1959) were followed by intensive " edification activities " in order to instil " revolutionary awareness " among those influenced by the purged elements.[39]

North Korean publications of the past few years have been exuberant in asserting the success of the collectivisation programme and the continuous increase (except in 1959 when the total output declined below the 1958 level) in agricultural production. The Seven-Year Development Plan (1961–67) calls for an increase of total agricultural production by 2·4 times, although the grain output is aimed at 1·7 times the 1960 norm. The plan calls for 5,000,000 metric tons of grain in 1963.[40] Obviously some progress has been made in agricultural production during the last several years, although the food problem in North Korea is far from being solved.

As of the spring of 1963, there is no sign of retreat in the North Korean collectivisation programme in spite of the virtual abandonment of the commune system in China. According to official sources, 1962 was another " bumper crop year " despite drought and floods. Is there

[36] *Cho Chung Ch'inson Nongop Hyoptong Chohap . . .*, p. 241.
[37] *Ibid.* p. 237.
[38] *Ibid.* p. 240.
[39] *Ibid.*
[40] See *Control Figures for the Seven-Year Plan (1961–67) for the Development of the National Economy of the Democratic People's Republic of Korea* (Pyongyang: Korean Central News Agency, 1961), p. 18. The officially reported grain outputs in 1960 and 1961 were 3,803,000 tons and 4,830,000 tons, respectively. Approximately 40 per cent. of the total was rice. The adjusted estimates of the U.S. Department of State for these years were 2,781,000 tons and 3,378,000 tons, respectively. See Department of State, Bureau of Intelligence and Research, " Research Memorandum," RSB-105, June 21, 1962, p. 11.

anything inherently superior in the North Korean system *vis-à-vis* the Chinese? Space does not permit detailed analysis of this question but a few factors are obviously in favour of North Korea: smaller territory (46,539 sq. mi. vs. 3,691,502 sq. mi. in China), smaller population (10,700,000 vs. 700,000,000 in China), relatively abundant supply of chemical fertilisers, and extensive irrigation facilities. The fact that the North Korean collectivisation programme was instituted immediately after a devastating war during which a great proportion of farmers had been uprooted from their farms and many others had abandoned their farms to flee to South Korea was also advantageous to the initial stage of collectivisation.

The success of agricultural policies in North Korea is not to be measured by the increase in production alone, however. As has been repeatedly emphasised by North Korean authorities, the major purpose of the socialisation movement has been to bring about the equilibrium between the industrial and agricultural sectors of the economy and to prepare the peasants for the transition to the Communist stage. Judged by this criterion, the land reform programme before the war was an obvious failure. But will collectivisation and intensive indoctrination successfully bring about a change in the minds of the peasants? Will the change be significant enough to avoid the kind of catastrophic defeat that the Communist régime suffered in 1950 with the mass exodus of the peasants? No one, including the Communist leaders themselves, can offer a definite answer to this question. One thing, however, is certain. The Communist régime will never be able to win over the minds of the peasants as long as it regards the rural population as a means to an end rather than an end in itself. As the Communist leaders should know, the Korean peasants have been exploited far too long not to recognise exploitation for what it is, no matter what it is called.

North Korea's Agricultural Development during the Post-War Period

By YOON T. KUARK *

IT is important to know the structure of the Korean economy prior to the division of the country in order to understand agricultural development in North Korea in terms of its capital expenditure and output during the post-war period.

During the first quarter of the twentieth century the Korean economy was based on agriculture. With over 70 per cent. of the population on the land until the end of the Second World War, agriculture has been the most important factor in Korea's economic life.[1] Handicraft provided only the most meagre standard of living. Two decades ago Korea was the world's fourth largest rice producer. Rice comprised about 60 per cent. of all crops. Others were barley, wheat, soyabeans, red-beans, peppers and potatoes. Special crops included cotton, tobacco, hemp and ginseng.

The significant growth of industry (mostly in North Korea) during the last three decades has transformed Korea's economy to that of an agrarian-industrial nation[2]—the predominantly agricultural economy of South Korea complementing that of the relatively industrialised North.[3]

* This is an excerpt and updating from the basic research on North and South Korea's Economic Development which was done during the 1960–61 academic year for the Economic Development Workshop Seminar at the University of Minnesota. The author is indebted to Professors M. Bronfenbrenner, J. Schmookler, Anne O. Krueger and fellow members of the Workshop for their valuable comments and suggestions. The author wishes to express thanks to Professor Bronfenbrenner for his help in obtaining microfilm data on North Korea from the U.S. Library of Congress, and also to Mrs. Elizabeth B. Green at the University of Denver for correcting the author's English. Errors and mistakes are the author's own responsibility.

1 Even in 1956 the farm population in North Korea was reported to comprise 56·6% of its population of about 10 million, and in 1960, 44·4% (see *Facts About Korea* [Pyongyang: Foreign Languages Publishing House, 1961], p. 9), while in South Korea nearly 63% of its population of about 22 million was engaged in agriculture in 1956 and about 58% in 1960. See *Economic Statistics Yearbook 1961* (Seoul: Bank of Korea), p. 138 and *Monthly Economic Research* (Seoul), March 1961, p. 220.

2 Zaichikov, V. T., *Geography of Korea*, translated into English by A. Parry. (New York: Institute of Pacific Relations, 1952), pp 52–53.

3 McCune, G. M. and Grey, A. L., *Korea Today* (Cambridge, Mass.: Harvard Un. Press, 1950), pp. 56–57. Figures available for the later years of the Japanese occupation show that while the North accounted for 86% of Korea's output in the heavy industry sector, the South was the source of about 75% of total production in light industry (food processing, textile and other consumer goods) sector.

The South supplied rice, barley, and many finished consumer goods to the North in exchange for fertilisers, power, fuel, lumber and metals. Therefore, the division of the country at the 38th parallel in 1945 was a crippling blow to the integrated functioning of the two halves of the economy.

After land reform during the period of 1945–47, the rural economy of North Korea made rapid progress, although its tempo lagged far behind that of industrial development. However, progress came to a halt during the Korean war. Agricultural land was devastated, partly because of bombardment, but also because of dislocation and the consequent poor attention given to crops.[4] Following the Korean war, the agricultural policy of the Communist Party and its government was directed toward two goals: (1) The swift reconstruction and rehabilitation of the war-shattered factories making agricultural implements, and of farms and irrigation systems so as to increase grain production and meet the pent-up demand for food. The development of livestock, vegetable and fruit production and sericulture was also an urgent necessity; (2) the rapid socialisation of agriculture by means of collectivisation. The Communist government hastened forward with agricultural co-operativisation. By August 1958, it was reported that complete co-operativisation had been achieved.

Capital Expenditures and Mechanisation

The total amount of state investment in the North during the Three-Year Plan (1954–56) period reached 7,400 million Won in old currency (before the currency reform of February 1959 when 100 old Won were exchanged for one new Won). Over half the money, 4,200 million old Won, went on irrigation and river dyke projects. This investment was a decisive factor in increasing grain production, providing as it did for adding 123,000 *chongbo* (one *chongbo* is 2·45 acres) of arable land and for building dykes capable of protecting 160,000 *chongbo*. Besides, in 1957 the government spent 1,400 million old Won on rural construction. During the four years from 1954 to 1957, the land under irrigation increased from 227,000 *chongbo* to 384,000, and the proportion of irrigated rice paddies to the total area of paddies increased from 39 per cent. to 77 per cent.[5]

[4] According to the North Korean régime " the damage inflicted upon the (North Korean) economy by the war amounted to 420,000 million (old) Won [approximately $3,000 million]." See *Post-war Rehabilitation and Development of the National Economy in the Democratic People's Republic of Korea* (Pyongyang: Foreign Languages Publishing House, 1957), p. 75. See also *Kyongje Konsol* (Pyongyang) May 1957, p. 5.

[5] JPRS, *Economic and Statistical Information on North Korea*, JPRS 901-D, Jan. 15, 1960, p. 79.

During the Three-Year Plan period, the area under rice cultivation increased by 61,000 *chongbo* (20·4 per cent. in 1956 against 16 per cent. in 1949 of total sown area) and that under corn by 367,000 *chongbo* (25·5 per cent. against 11·8 per cent.). By the end of the Three-Year Plan (1956), grain harvested amounted to 2,870,000 tons, "exceeding by far the highest production figure of the pre-war days." It is claimed that during the subsequent First Five-Year Plan grain output was increased enough to make the country self-sufficient. Cultivation of industrial crops and oil-bearing plants has been expanded due to the rapidly increasing demands of light industry, and every year ginned cotton and other materials are imported. Fruit-growing acreage amounting to 100,000 *chongbo* was newly brought under cultivation. It is reported that the total capital expenditures for increasing agricultural output during 1954 to 1959 amounted to 23,900 million Won (equivalent to 239 million new Won).[6]

It is known that state farms played an important part in introducing mechanisation and advanced farming methods. Widely introduced methods included rice seeding on cold beds or dry fields, wide row and criss-cross sowing, use of an excellent quality of seeds and increased supplies of chemical fertilisers.[7] Chemical fertilisers used in 1953 were about 30,000 tons, and by 1959 use was increased to 310,000 tons, approximately 172 kg. per *chongbo* of arable land.[8] It was reported that there were 15 machine-service stations dealing with 500 tractors of 15 horse-power, and tilling 95,000 *chongbo* in 1953. With help from the Agricultural Research Institute under the Academy of Science, and from agricultural colleges, some 50 machine-service stations handled, by 1957, 2,092 tractors (15 horsepower), tilling 854,000 *chongbo* (19 per cent. of total arable land) and supplied other advanced farm machines and implements such as weeding machines and seeders, threshing machines and fan-blowers. By 1959 the machine-service stations increased to 84 units, the number of tractors to 8,050 (15 horsepower), and the volume of various machine work by 2·9 times over that of 1953.[9]

It is also reported that the electrification of co-operative farms has become extensive, and that in 1959 more than 7,000 generators, motors and transformers were supplied to the farms. In view of the rich hydro-electric power resources available in North Korea, these figures appear to be conceivable.

6 *North Korea's Economic Development Since Liberation* (Japanese edition) (Pyongyang: Foreign Languages Publishing House, 1960), pp. 25–26.

7 JPRS 901-D, *op. cit.*, pp. 80–82.

8 *North Korea's Economic Development Since Liberation, op. cit.*, p. 26.

9 *Ibid.* p. 26.

AGRICULTURAL PRODUCTION

Following the complete shut-off of economic intercourse between the North and the South after the birth of the South Korean Government in 1948, an acute shortage of foodstuffs in North Korea occurred, and remained a perennial problem for the Communist régime thereafter. This was the basic reason for the enormous capital expenditures ploughed into agriculture during the immediate post-Second World War period.[10] The land reform in 1945–47 and the co-operativisation immediately following the Korean War were typically Communist attempts to increase agricultural production through rigid control, and to siphon off as much of that output as possible to pay for industrialisation. This was effected through heavy taxes.

A very interesting feature of the agricultural co-operatives of North Korea is the device of " efficient division of labour " of farm workers, that is, the work-team system. In co-operative farms there are three types of work-teams—specialised, mixed, and all-purpose—each work-team consisting of from a dozen to 100 workers, depending upon its type of work. A specialised work-team specialises either in one crop (such as a " rice work-team " or a " cotton work-team ") or in one species of livestock (such as a " dairy-cow work-team " or a " sheep work-team ") at farms where a great number of livestock are raised. A mixed work-team raises more than one crop or more than one species of livestock, for instance, an " agricultural team " which raises both rice and vegetables, or a " livestock team " which raises both dairy-cows and hogs. An all-purpose work-team is engaged in more than one sector of agriculture, such as raising hogs or poultry, cultivating fodder fields, or engaging in pomiculture, crop raising, etc., concurrently.[11]

All these types of work-teams have their strong points and drawbacks. Because a team can concentrate on its specialised work, it can be very efficient in terms of labour productivity. However, the work-team organisation can create a great many problems in determining optimal team size, classification of mediocre workers' specialisation,

[10] However, in the later years, especially after the Korean War, state investment in agriculture was reduced. The ratio of capital expenditures between industry and agriculture to the total are shown as follows. From the table one can easily see that the Communist régime put far more emphasis on developing industry than on agriculture in the post-Korean War period. The data below are in percentages.

	1954	1955	1956	1957	1958
Industry	43·2	51·4	53·6	57.9	54.6
Agriculture	6·4	10·5	10·5	5.1	7.7
Others	50·4	38·1	35·9	37.0	37·7

Source: JPRS 901-D, *op. cit.*, p. 222.

[11] *Kyongje Chisik*, No. 2, February 1960, pp. 11–13. *Kyongje Chisik*, No. 4, April 1960, pp. 24–28.

distribution of adequate tools and implements, work norms, production plan assignments, etc. In fact, Premier Kim Il-song deplored the unsatisfactory performance of work-teams and suggested various solutions to these problems in his speech at the Chongsanni general meeting of the Communist Party in late 1959.[12]

The incentive system employed by the Communist régime is also worth studying. Each work-team operates on its own independent accounting system [13] whose balance sheet indicates the team's performance and supplies the yardstick for material reward and preferential treatment by the Communist Party.[14] Incentives for overfulfilment of state production plans in farm, livestock and sericulture output are given up to 40 per cent. of excess production in the form of products or cash or grain; penalties for failure to fulfil the plans are imposed in terms of products or cash or grain between 10 and 20 per cent. of the deficit production. The head of an agricultural work-team receives an additional reward of 10–20 per cent. of the reward given to him as a team member if his team has overfulfilled its production plan.

In the case of agricultural products, the incentives and penalties are applied to the individual work-teams. If a work-team grows more than one crop, it will receive rewards for those crops whose output has surpassed the assigned production plan; but the work-team must pay a penalty on the other crops whose output falls short of the production target. The penalties for deficit output of products of all types are added to the co-operative's collective income.[15]

A work-team must fulfil not only monthly production plans but also daily and ten-day production plans. Specific measures concerning production plan implementation are taken by the Party as a result of analysis of so-called " production rhythm assurance." [16] Thus, a work-team must always maintain its " rhythm " of production performance

[12] *Ibid*. No. 2, February 1960, pp. 11–13. See also JPRS, *Economic Report on North Korea* (No. 29 of series), Aug. 15, 1960, pp. 81–86.

[13] The work-team is not authorised to reduce or increase the use of labour, nor to buy or sell intermediate goods or raw materials. These are supplied by the higher echelon organs. It is not in a position to prepare a complete profit and loss statement, because it is not even allowed to open its own settlement account. The team just prepares its balance sheet for plan fulfilment within the limit of given factors of production, wage funds and budgets. *Ibid*. No. 4, April 1960, pp. 11–14.

[14] In this connection, the Ministry of Agriculture published " Standard Regulations Concerning Material Preferential Treatment and Indemnities," *ibid*. pp. 11–14. See also JPRS, *Economic Report on North Korea* (31st of series), Oct. 14, 1960, pp. 88–90.

[15] Ahn Chae-bok, " Material Incentives and Penalties in Agricultural Co-operatives," *Kyongje Konsol*, No. 10, October 1959, pp. 34–37. See also JPRS, *Economic Report on North Korea* (No. 23 of series) Feb. 25, 1960, pp. 31–32.

[16] *Kyongje Chisik*, No. 1, January 1960, pp. 47–48. See also JPRS, *Economic Report on North Korea* (No. 28 of series) July 25, 1960, pp. 5–10.

or pace of work, under the slogan "Let us produce more with existing labour and facilities." [17]

A Communist Party official, Kim Kin-am, declared that "the introduction of the independent accounting system in work-teams, and the work-team bonus system, revision of wage schedule of workers in machine-service stations, improvement in the purchasing system, increase in the purchasing price of livestock products, and abolition of tax-in-kind for agricultural co-operatives in mountainous regions . . . have created great incentives for agricultural labour as well as for the increase of agricultural productivity." [18]

However, it is interesting to note that the average output of principal product per *chongbo* indicates that agricultural productivity has not quite caught up to the pre-Korean War level even in 1957, which was termed a record year or a "turning-point" in the First Five-Year Plan period.[19] It is a moot question whether alleged productivity in agriculture has actually increased so remarkably between 1958 and 1960, a period for which no verifiable data are available to this author.

Table 1. Average Per Chongbo Output of Principal Produce
(In tons)

	1946	1949	1953	1954	1955	1956	1957
Rice	2·71	3·03	2·84	2·27	2·73	2·82	2·92
Corn	0·90	1·33	0·93	1·30	1·08	1·25	1·49
Vegetables ...	8·67	17·50	9·71	11·61	12·92	14·63	16·32
Potatoes ...	4·24	5·92	4·39	6·74	6·36	7·32	7·11

Source: JPRS, 901–D, p. 210.

Let us now turn our attention to the actual achievement in agricultural production during the post-Korean War period. More or less confirmable figures, available to this author only up to 1957, are shown in the following tables. The figures themselves show that increase in agricultural production has not been so phenomenal, unlike the Communist régime's impressive (although unconfirmed) percentage ratios over the years.

[17] *Ibid.* pp. 9–12.

[18] Kim Kin-am, "Life of the People under the Socialist System," *Kulloja*, No. 6, June 1960, pp. 24–33. See also JPRS, *Economic Report on North Korea* (31st of series) Oct. 14, 1960, p. 88.

[19] *Chosen Chungang Nyongam 1958* (Pyongyang), December 1958, pp. 102–137. See also JPRS, *Economic and Statistical Information on North Korea,* 901-D, pp. 79–104.

Table 2. Total Value of Grain Output of North Korea

	Total area sown (thousand *chongbo*)	Index	Total grain output* (thousand tons)	Index	Annual growth rate
1953 ...	2,295	100	2,327	100	——
1954 ...	2,337	102	2,230	96	−4·2%
1955 ...	2,325	97	2,340	101	4·9%
1956 ...	2,413	105	2,873	123	22·8%
1957 ...	2,555	113	3,201	138	11·4%
1958 ...	N.A.	N.A.	3,700	159	15·6%

* Total grain output includes all food grains such as rice, barley, wheat, corn, foxtail millet, broomcorn millet and beans, etc.

Source: *Economic and Statistical Information on North Korea*, JPRS 901-D, Jan. 15, 1960, pp. 83–85. Also *Nodong Shinmun* (*Labour News*), Jan. 19, 1958, and other North Korean periodicals.

Table 3. Total Output of Agricultural Produce
(thousand tons)

	1949	1953	1954	1955	1956	1957
Food grain	2,654	2,327	2,230	2,340	2,873	3,201
Rice	1,158	1,229	1,025	1,242	1,392	1,459
Corn	375	224	307	361	760	1,130
Wheat and Barley ...	212	162	196	197	183	164
Foxtail millet ...	394	268	273	222	117	58
Broomcorn millet ...	103	87	87	95	71	58
Soybeans	191	208	196	128	230	206
Others	221	149	146	95	120	126
Tobacco	10	2	6	7	12	13
Vegetables	797	466	833	954	1,049	1,249
Tubers	782	412	647	619	948	1,186
Potatoes	616	344	500	512	761	965
Fodder crops	7	17	42	64	72	81
Others	159	51	105	43	115	140

Source: JPRS 901-D, p. 207.

Table 4. Number of Livestock (Year-end Census)
(in head)

	1946	1949	1953	1956	1957
Milk cow	766	959	637	1,205	2,851
Korean cattle ...	470,978	786,765	503,761	483,619	566,303
Horse	9,628	8,787	6,367	15,028	12,416
Sheep and goats ...	6,913	12,696	25,286	87,516	121,651
Hogs	219,847	659,645	542,725	710,314	1,339,351

Source: JPRS 901-D, p. 216.

Agricultural output has risen at an average annual growth rate of 10·1 per cent. during the post-Korean War period, except for 1954. The proportion of total value of agricultural product to national income, compared with that of industrial product, has declined in recent years, as might be expected in the course of industrialisation.

Table 5. Proportion of National Income by Sectors

	Agricultural output	Industrial output*
1949	53·5%	46·7%
1956	39·9	60·1
1957	36·6	63·4
1958	31·4	68·6
1959	30·0	70·0

*Industrial output here includes all non-agricultural output excluding " Service."

Source: Kim Sung-jun, "The Two-Horse March Demands the Full-Scale Assistance of Industry to Agriculture," *Kulloja*, No. 6, June 1960, pp. 18–23. See also, JPRS, *Economic Report on North Korea* (No. 31 of series) Oct. 14, 1960, p. 14.

It is very interesting at this point to make some comparison of agricultural production between North and South Korea. Comparative economic factors relevant to agriculture in 1957 were as follows.[20]

	North	South
Area—square miles ..	47,097	37,959
Paddy fields—acres ..	1,140,475	2,936,697
Dry fields—acres	3,773,245	1,984,047
Population—persons ..	10,000,000	22,500,000

As of 1957, *per capita* production of rice in the North was approximately 150 kg. against South Korea's 110 kg.; wheat and barley 16 kg. for the North against 15 kg. for the South. It is apparent from the following table that South Korea enjoys far more grain production than North Korea, and yet its *per capita* figures are less favourable than those of the North because of the relative population size.

Table 6. Comparison of Selected Agricultural Production
(in thousand metric tons)

	1954		1955		1956		1957	
	North	*South*	*North*	*South*	*North*	*South*	*North*	*South*
Rice	1,025	2,295	1,242	2,374	1,392	1,955	1,459	2,408
Wheat and Barley	196	455	197	387	183	402	164	366
Corn	307	11·8	361	12·5	760	10·5	1,130	13·0

Note: South Korea's figures for agricultural products are published in terms of *sok*, which is equivalent to about 4·96 bushels or 180·39

[20] Refer to McCune, S., " Korea: Geographical Parallels, 1950–60," *The Journal of Geography*, No. 5, May 1960, p. 204.

litres. I computed South Korea's figures in metric tons, using the following conversion rates: 1 bushel of hulled rice=68 lbs. (a bushel of unhulled rice=45 lbs. and 152 lbs. of unhulled rice is equivalent to 100 lbs. of hulled rice); 1 bushel of wheat=60 lbs.; 1 bushel of barley=48 lbs.; 1 bushel of corn=56 lbs., and 1 metric ton= 2,204·6 lbs.

Source: North Korea's figures: *Economic and Statistical Information on North Korea*, JPRS 901-D, Jan. 15, 1960, p. 169. South Korea's figures: *Annual Economic Review*, 1959 (Seoul : Bank of Korea, 1959), pp. (III)–147–148.

However, it is very intriguing to compare my figures of *per capita* food grain output and those of the Communist Party official, Kim Kin-am, published in *Kulloja* (*Working People*) under the heading, " The Share Per Member Family of Agricultural Co-operatives," as follows:

	1955	1956	1957	1958
Food grain crops (kg.) ...	1,250	1,616	1,742	1,826
Tubers (kg.)	193	357	434	501
Cash (in new Won) ...	56·05	95·42	137·03	203·50

Source: Kim Kin-am, " Life of the People under the Socialist System," *Kulloja*, No. 6, June 1960, pp. 24–33.

My calculations show that *per capita* food grains for 1957 were approximately 280 kgs. (rice, wheat, barley and corn) while Kim's *per co-operative family* food grain crop was 1,742 kgs.; the average family size of North Korean co-operatives should not exceed five persons (280 kgs. × 5 = 1,400 kgs.).

FLYING HORSE MOVEMENT

Although agricultural collectivisation in North Korea was carried out along the lines of the Soviet example,[21] Chinese innovations in agriculture inspired the North Koreans. The Ch'ollima Undong (Flying Horse Movement)[22] was launched in September 1958, only a few months after the start of the Great Leap Forward in China.

[21] Kim Il-song wrote for *Pravda* in October 1957 that " experience in agricultural co-operativisation in the Soviet Union became the guiding compass of our Party's agricultural co-operativisation policies." Kim Il-song, *Selected Works, V* (1960), p. 209. The North Koreans have always used the term " hyopdong-wha (co-operativisation) " instead of " Kongdong-wha (collectivisation) " in agriculture.

[22] The direct translation is *Thousand-ri Horse Movement* (one *ri* equals about one-third of a mile). The flying horse image was perhaps taken from a popular Korean legendary novel about ancient China, The *Samguk Chi* (Tales of the Three Kingdoms). See Paige, Glenn D., " Building Socialism in North Korea: The Emergence of the ' Korean Model ' " (Mimeograph), Princeton University, 1962, p. 13. The Chinese influence in North Korea was perhaps most pronounced in 1958, as Chinese innovation and assertiveness in building socialism were hailed in North Korea, a Sino-Korean friendship association was established in that October, and the Chinese Volunteers' Army withdrew at the end of the year.

Some Chinese farming techniques, notably in rice cultivation (such as seeding on cold beds and dry fields, wide row and criss-cross sowing, etc.) were adopted. Communal cooking and other " socialist " measures suggested Chinese influence. The North Korean Communists were neither attracted to the Chinese notions of communal dwelling nor to those of making " every man a soldier," apparently because of North Korea's shortage of labour.

Another innovation perhaps inspired by China's experience was the integration of 16,032 agricultural co-operatives into 3,843 economic-administrative units into the *ri* (an administrative unit below *Kun* or county) levels which took place in October 1958. Since 1959, the North Koreans seem to have been cautious about the Chinese communes. The kitchen plots, chickens, ducks, pigs, rabbits and so forth have been restored to private hands.[23] The individual peasant is told to produce and sell more of these products so that he can earn money to build a new house.[24] North Korea has returned to the Leninist line in agriculture: " electrification and mechanisation," supplemented by the Asian slogan of " irrigation." In early 1962 neither the Chinese people's communes nor the " three red banners " were being hailed in North Korea.[25]

The Flying Horse Movement appears to have been more significant in heavy industry than in agriculture. The continued emphasis on expanding heavy industry seriously tightened the economic bottleneck in 1959. Although the targets of the Five-Year Plan were said to have been achieved by mid-1959, the undue concentration on heavy industry had been a drain on the rural labour force, and therefore aggravated the serious imbalance between agriculture and industry. The impact was severe, if not disastrous. No wonder Kim Il-song had to put so much emphasis on quickly mechanising agriculture and on increasing the productivity of labour. Hence, the 1960 slogan of " Let us fulfil the task of the shock absorption period." This may explain why the figures of total food grain output for 1959 are not shown in the *Central Yearbook* for 1960, while the absolute figures for sericultural output, vegetable and fruit output, number of livestock, etc., are published.

For attacking Kim's undue concentration on heavy industry in the Five-Year Plan, both Pak Chang-ok, Soviet-Korean director of the Central Statistical Commission and Choe Chang-ik, leading Yenan Communist in North Korea and their followers were purged in late

23 Narumoto, K., " Political Story," *Kita-Chosen no Kiroku* (Record of North Korea), Tokyo: Shindokusho-sha, 1960, p. 67.

24 Korean Workers' Party. *Problems Concerning the Political and Economic Strengthening of the Agricultural Co-operatives*, Pyongyang: KWP Press, 1960, p. 190.

25 Paige, Glenn D., *op. cit.*, p. 14.

1958. Kim Il-song reportedly said in October 1959, " if our Party had listened to their views we would not have reached today's level of industrial development in fifty years." [26] Apparently, Kim must have felt the need to vindicate his position. In the first four years of the Seven-Year Plan (1961–67) there is to be virtually no new heavy industrial construction. Electrification and mechanisation are emphasised, together with extensive irrigation and use of fertilisers to increase agricultural production.

In 1962, 5 million tons of food grain were to be produced. However, the actual fulfilment figures are not known. The inconsistency of what published figures there are casts doubt on the fulfilment of the Plan although the mechanisation of agriculture was apparently rather impressive. Twenty-seven more machine service stations were added in 1961. They are said to have used 15,700 tractors of 15 horsepower and supplied 622,000 tons of various chemical fertilisers in 1962.

CONCLUSIONS

In his report before the National Conference of Agricultural Co-operatives in 1959, Premier Kim Il-song stated: " In the past our agriculture concentrated itself upon increasing the production of food grains, and yet the results were not too satisfactory. . . ." On the reorganisation of the agricultural structure, he said: " The Party policy of giving priority to food grain production and concurrently expanding other sectors of agriculture such as industrial crops, livestock, sericulture, pomiculture and fisheries should be continuously and thoroughly implemented. Thus, our countryside should be built up into a strong raw material base as well as a strong food-supply base." [27] I think this statement well summarises North Korea's agricultural development during the post-war period, although what " should be " is quite different from what " is." North Korea can hardly reach the production level of rice, barley and wheat of the naturally fertile land of South Korea as a whole, just as the converse may be true with respect to heavy industry.

There is no doubt that agricultural collectivisation, sanctioned by Marxist-Leninist principles, has made possible the large increase in agricultural production. With its rigorous regimentation, over 95 per cent. of the peasants are herded into Soviet-style co-operatives, and toil 12 to 14 hours (48 legal working hours per week plus various chores

[26] Kim Il-song, *Let Us Grasp the Central Link and Concentrate All Our Forces in Solving All Problems*, Pyongyang: KWP Press, 1959, p. 12.

[27] *Kyongje Konsol*, No. 11, November 1959, pp. 7–13. See also JPRS, *Economic Report on North Korea* (24th of series), p. 58.

within the co-operatives) per day under the "big-brothers" supervision and "self-criticism" report system. However, the Communists' claim that self-sufficiency in agricultural production was attained by 1959 is quite untenable in view of the fact that rationing of foodstuffs is still in force and troubles permeate the collective mess halls,[28] and that there is no evidence of food-grain export.[29]

28 So Shin Song, "Problems in Connection with the Organisation and Operation of Mess Halls for Families and Unmarried Persons," *Sangop*, No. 7, July 1960, p. 8–11.

29 *Kyongje Chisik*, No. 3, March 1960, Editorial titled "Let us Acquire More and Save More Foreign Exchange," pp. 2–4. Also refer to *Vneshnyaya Torgovlya (Foreign Trade)* (Moscow), No. 9, 1958, cited by Karshinov, L. N., in his *People's Democratic Republic of Korea*, JPRS 3822, Sept. 6, 1960, pp. 68–69.

The Judicial and Administrative Structure in North Korea *

By ILPYONG J. KIM

A KNOWLEDGE of judicial and administrative structure plays a vital part in understanding the government and politics of any society. In a Communist society, the administrative apparatus plays an important role, not only in controlling the society but also in implementing Party and government directives. To fully understand the government and politics of North Korea, it may prove helpful to investigate the administrative structure by which the North Korean leaders control the society and remain in power. After a decade and a half of political rule, these North Korean leaders are faced with constant social changes and rising pressures from below. The relations between political power and political institutions, between political ideal and social reality, between the formulation and implementation of policy, have in fact been a major ideological concern for North Korea's administrators, a preoccupation they share with the leaders of other Communist societies. The amount of information made available about the North Korean judicial and administrative system has been scanty at best. This article therefore is exploratory and not definitive in nature. By utilising the materials that are available this article attempts to present North Korean views and attitudes about law and administration, and to describe the institutional framework in which the legal and administrative apparatus functions; at the same time it also attempts to examine the Soviet and Communist Chinese impact on the development of North Korea's administrative system.

North Korean jurists and text writers have testified to the great influence of Soviet legal theory and practice on the basic structure of the North Korean state. Law, for North Korean leaders, has simply been an instrument of politics; for as Lenin once wrote in describing his Bolshevik régime, " dictatorship is power based directly upon force and unrestricted by any laws." [1] North Korean views on law and state are an outgrowth of the Marxist conception of history and the class

* The author wishes to express his appreciation to Professor John N. Hazard of Columbia University who read this paper and made useful comments.

[1] John N. Hazard, *Law and Social Change in the U.S.S.R.* (London: Stevens, 1953), p. 1.

struggle, in which all forms of law and the state are considered to be forever contaminated by prior association with the bourgeoisie. Following the liberation of Korea from Japanese occupation, a fresh theoretical formulation of the nature of law became a part of North Korea's public policy. According to a North Korean work on law, " the Korean people completely destroyed Japanese law and colonial institutions. Law under Japanese domination had been the reflection of the ruler's will and had been utilised as a powerful instrument to maintain imperialist rule." [2] This writer asserted that the destruction of the old law had been more thorough in North Korea than in East European countries, and he therefore argued that the new legal system established in North Korea possessed the characteristics of socialist law.

The North Korean jurists foresaw that law and the state would ultimately wither away, but at the present stage these institutions were to be strengthened and given a special place: this conception of law was in fact similar to that of the Soviet Union in the era of Stalin. These jurists were compelled to recognise that law was subordinate to the politics and class interest of the state. Addressing the national conference for prosecutors and judicial administrators in 1958, Premier Kim Il-song asserted: " The law in our country is an instrument of state policy. Since our state policy is our Party policy those who do not understand our Party policy cannot serve in the legal professions of our country." [3] Thus, an understanding of the Party line is more important to North Korean jurists than the learning of legal codes or practice. Law in North Korea is held to have a positive role in the development of socialism. Since it is a constructive force for building the new order, law is considered necessary in the period of transition to Communism. The Soviet definition, that law is the " totality (a) of the rules of conduct, expressing the will of the dominant class and established in legal order, and (b) of customs and rules of community life sanctioned by state authority . . . and agreeable to the dominant class," [4] is well accepted and frequently discussed by North Korean jurists.

As in other fields of the Communist system, the economic theme has been predominant in the courts and adjudications. Even before North Korea drafted its Constitution, such laws as the Land Reform (March 5, 1946), the Labour Law (June 24, 1946), and the Law on Nationalisation

[2] *Urinara Popui Palchon* (*The Development of Law in Our Country*) (Pyongyang: State Publishing House, 1960), p. 10. This book is a collection of six essays by North Korean jurists on such specialised fields as civil law, land law, law of the agricultural co-operatives, labour law, criminal law, and procedural law.

[3] Kim Il-song, " For the Execution of Our Party's Judicial Policy," *Kim Il-song Sonjip* (*Selected Works of Kim Il-song*) (Pyongyang: Worker's Daily Press, 1960), V, 1960, p. 450.

[4] Andrei Y. Vyshinsky, *The Law of the Soviet State*, translated by Hugh W. Babb (New York: The Macmillan Company, 1948), p. 50.

of Industry (August 10, 1946) had been proclaimed.[5] These laws appeal to the majority of the population just as the laws of the Soviet government had appealed to the Russians after the revolution. The general framework contained in these Korean laws followed the general pattern laid down in similar Soviet legislation. The Constitution of the Korean People's Democratic Republic also put a strong emphasis on the economic structure of the country.

According to Articles 82 to 94 of the Constitution, judicial and supervisory powers are concentrated in two government organs: the Supreme People's Court, which is the highest organ with supervisory powers over local and special courts; and the Supreme Prosecutor-General, who has supreme supervisory powers over all ministries of government, the local people's prosecutors at all levels, and the people at large. In addition to these organs, the cabinet, as an executive branch of the government, has a wide range of power to maintain public order. The Ministry of Internal Affairs, under the cabinet, is in charge of the police force to maintain public security as well as to control the vast network of the secret police.

In March 1950, the Supreme People's Assembly of the Korean People's Democratic Republic adopted the "Law Governing the Organisation of the Courts in the Republic." [6] This law provides for the establishment of a three-level court system; the Supreme Court at the top, the provincial courts in the middle, and people's courts in the cities, counties or districts. The primary aim of the courts and the Procuracy is to guarantee the strict enforcement of laws. The tasks of the courts are to protect the people's state and social system by law from all encroachments; to protect state and public property, and the rights and interests of state organs, state-owned enterprises, co-operative organisations and citizens; and to guarantee the strict observance and execution of state laws by state organs, government employees and citizens. It is also emphasised that the courts apply a penalty to a criminal not merely to punish him but also to re-educate him. By drawing the masses into court proceedings, the courts attempt to foster the law-abiding spirits of citizens and enhance the educational role of trials. Such trials place special emphasis on loyalty to the state and people, on accurate execution of the law, on the protection of state and public property, and on love for labour and respect for public order.

[5] These laws will be translated and included in the author's forthcoming book *Communism in North Korea: A Documentary History.*

[6] *Choson Minjujui Inmin Kongwhakuk Poplyong mit Choeko Inminhwoei Sangim Wiwonhwoe Chonglyongjip* (*Collected Laws of the Korean People's Democratic Republic and Decrees of the Presidium of the Supreme People's Assembly*) (Pyongyang: Presidium of the Supreme People's Assembly, 1955), I, p. 30.

A court in most first-instance proceedings consists of one judge and two people's assessors; in some special cases, however, which are defined by law, a court is composed of three professional judges.[7] Official writers have asserted that courts and judges in North Korea are " independent and subject only to the law " (Constitution, Article 88). Any citizen who has the right to vote can be elected to the office of judge or assessor; those who served as judges or prosecutors under Japanese rule, however, are not permitted to run for office. All judges are to be elected by secret ballot at each level of the legislative system; Supreme Court judges are elected by the Supreme People's Assembly for a term of three years, judges of the provincial courts are elected by the Provincial People's Assembly, also for a term of three years, and judges of the city or county people's courts are elected by the local people's councils for a term of two years. All these judges are subject to recall by the organ which elects them and all courts are to be guided and controlled by the next court above. Critics of the North Korean system have pointed out that since the judges are either members of the Worker's (Communist) Party or are controlled by it, they are no longer independent judges but are instruments of the Korean Worker's Party.

The people's court in cities and county (or district) is a tribunal of original jurisdiction with competence to try a wide variety of civil and criminal cases. It tries to settle disputes dealing with property, the violation of labour laws, divorce and payment of alimony, and inheritance, etc. In criminal matters, the court tries cases against persons accused of stealing from the state and co-operative properties, crimes against persons, damage to private property, negligence in official duty and business management, and crimes concerning public health and safety.[8]

The courts at the intermediate level (cities, counties and districts) hear appeals from the lower courts and have original jurisdiction over important civil and criminal cases which are beyond the competence of the lower courts. The original jurisdiction of criminal cases includes such crimes as crimes against state authority,[9] against persons, state and co-operative property, and negligence in official duties; the jurisdiction in civil cases covers the disputes between North Korean citizens and foreigners. The intermediate courts are divided into two departments: civil and criminal. Each department consists of three judges who hear appeals from the lower courts in their specialised fields.

7 Article 17, " Law Governing the Organisation of the Courts."

8 For the criminal code and more specific provisions for economic crimes see " Criminal Legislation of the People's Democratic Republic of Korea," in M. A. Gel'fer, ed., *Ugolovnoye zakonodaltel'stvo zarbezhnykh sotsialistticheskikh gosudarstvo* (*Criminal Legislation in Foreign Socialist States*) (Moscow: State Publishing House of Juridical Literature, 1957), pp. 27–51.

9 *Ibid.* Chapter 13 (Arts. 64–81).

The highest tribunal in North Korea is the Supreme Court, which has broad powers to supervise the lower and intermediate courts within the republic. It can overrule any decision of the inferior courts, and it may remove a case from the jurisdiction of a lower court and assume jurisdiction itself.[10] The Supreme Court consists of the criminal, civil, and special collegiums. One judge and two people's assessors sit in each collegium which has jurisdiction over appeals from the appropriate department of the lower court. The president of the Supreme Court is authorised to sit and preside over all cases tried by the three collegiums.[11] Thus, the president of the highest tribunal can easily control any case on trial.

Cases decided by a collegium of the Supreme Court can be appealed to the plenary session of the Supreme Court, in which the judges of all three collegiums, the president of the Supreme Court, and the Prosecutor-General sit. This plenary session should be called no less than once every two months, and hears cases considered too important to be heard by the lower courts. Such cases are usually brought before this session by special request of the Prosecutor-General, the Minister of Internal Affairs, or high state organs, and mostly involve administrative crime committed by high-ranking officials of the republic. However, the highly publicised purge trial of Yi Song-yop, the Minister of Justice, and eleven other high-ranking government and Party officials in 1953, was conducted by a special military tribunal, which was set up for the purpose of this trial. They were accused of plotting to overthrow the government, but many observers interpreted this trial as an attempt to find scapegoats for the failure of the Korean War.

Besides the regular court system described above, North Korea has established a Special Court which is divided into two sections: a military court for the armed forces, and a transport court which has jurisdiction over crimes committed by the employees of the various transport systems. The president and judges of these special courts are appointed, rather than elected, by the president of the Supreme Court (formerly by the Minister of Justice), and assessors of these courts are elected by the employees of the organ in which the special courts are established. The military tribunal is set up not only in the divisional, corps and army headquarters of the armed forces, but it is also established in the organs of the Ministry of Internal Affairs. These special courts, military and transport, are supervised by the special collegium of the Supreme Court and they function independently of the military or administrative channel of command.

[10] Art. 48, " Law Governing the Organisation of the Courts."
[11] *Ibid.*, Art. 57.

One of the most unique and powerful agencies of North Korea's totalitarian system is the Procuracy, which is vested with supreme supervisory power to ensure the strict enforcement of law. Just like its Soviet counterpart the Procuracy is in practice " indissolubly associated with the directing organs of the Communist Party " [12] to which it is responsible. The constitution of the republic thus makes the Procuracy entirely independent of " any local organs whatsoever, being solely subordinate to the Prosecutor-General of the Korean People's Democratic Republic." [13] The Prosecutor-General is appointed rather than elected, by the Supreme People's Assembly and he, in turn, appoints prosecutors in the provinces, cities, and counties.

The Procuracy exercises its authority over all ministries of the cabinet, over all local organs of the state and persons working in these organs, and over the citizens at large. Prosecutors at all levels have the following duties: to check the decisions, decrees, and measures of state organs to ensure their conformity with the law; to inquire into criminal cases and to conduct prosecutions; to supervise the adjudication of the people's courts to ensure their conformity with the law; to supervise the execution of judgments and reform activities; and to exercise the right to prosecute or join in the prosecution of important civil cases involving the interest of the state and the people.

The Prosecutor-General's office is divided into six specialised departments: transport, people's army, internal, criminal, civil and special prosecutions. The prosecutors assigned to the Department of Special Prosecutions are mainly concerned with political crimes. Article 20 of the " Law Governing the Organisation of the Procuracy and Internal Affairs " can be applied to any person who is considered to be untrustworthy to the régime. This article provides for prosecution of such broad crimes as subversive conduct, anti-Soviet activities, subversive instigation, anti-Communist conduct, espionage, and association with subversive intent, etc.

The Procuracy and the apparatus of the Ministry of Internal Affairs are apparently linked closely with the coercion of the masses. The techniques applied by these two organs recall those of Stalin's secret police. The organisation of the secret police has been well documented by those who defected to the South during the Korean War and its aftermath. Such refugees from the North reported the existence of large-scale political terror used to eliminate the opposition. The North Korean press, however, has since given the impression that the North Korean leaders are gradually shifting their techniques of control from compulsion to persuasion as the régime consolidates its political power and

[12] Vyshinsky, *op. cit.*, pp. 525–526.
[13] Constitution, Art. 94.

rebuilds its economic base. Beginning in 1958, the tenth anniversary of the establishment of the republic, the régime has more than once called on Party cadres and government officials to penetrate the masses in order to indoctrinate and persuade them to accept Communist ideology and Party directives.

The Procuracy has the power to appeal against the decision of a court at any time. Since the Prosecutor-General participates in the plenary session of the Supreme Court he has the authority to issue directives to lower courts on judicial procedures. The prosecutor not only has broad authority over the administrative agencies but also serves as an agent to receive and process the complaints of ordinary citizens. Like his Soviet counterpart he is described as " the watchman of socialist legality." [14]

No judicial system exists in an administrative vacuum—least of all in a Communist state. North Korea's judicial system, considered by itself, is one specific mechanism by which the Party may control the people. But considered in the larger context of political administrative theory, it reflects the larger problems that exist in any totalitarian society where the few control the many. Those who are familiar with the post-war development of Soviet administration [15] will immediately notice its enormous impact on the administrative system in North Korea. The cabinet organisation in the formative stage after the war followed the Soviet pattern of small units. The first administrative organs established in North Korea consisted of only ten administrative bureaus which had large authority over the entire region of North Korea. These bureaus were: industry, transportation, agriculture and forestry, commerce, finance, postal administration, public safety, public health, education, and judicial administration.

The post-war trends towards unification and centralisation in the Soviet Union have been reflected in North Korea's own administration. By February 1946 the administrative units which were set up in the local regions had been consolidated to form the central administration. This organ was called the North Korean Provisional People's Committee. Lenin's argument that the government of the proletariat would gain strength from organising the local government so that the housewife might participate was taken into consideration in the formation of the

[14] Vyshinsky, *op. cit.*, p. 537.

[15] Writings on this aspect of the Soviet system are too numerous to illustrate here; however, the following articles present an excellent description of its development. John N. Hazard, " Political, Administrative and Judicial Structure in the U.S.S.R. since the War," *The Annals of the American Academy of Political and Social Science* (May 1949), and " Governmental Development in the U.S.S.R. since Stalin," *Annals* (January 1956), Merle Fainsod, " Recent Development in Soviet Public Administration," *Journal of Politics* (November 1949), Leonard Schapiro and S. V. Utechin, " Soviet Government Today," *The Political Quarterly* (April–June 1961).

North Korean administration. In November 1946 a general election was held to form a legislative body. By February 1947 the cabinet of the central government was established with the legal consent of the North Korean People's Assembly and took over the functions of the Provisional People's Committee. This cabinet consisted of thirteen ministries and four departments in addition to the posts of the premier and the three deputy premiers. A year later four more cabinet posts were added to the central government making a total of seventeen ministries.

The post-Korean War record gives the impression that public administrators in North Korea have been inclined to favour centralisation of administration to meet the needs of post-war reconstruction. Following the plenum of the Party's Central Committee in March 1954 the cabinet posts were reshuffled. Five young leaders in the party and government were elevated to the posts of deputy premiership.[16] According to the "Law Governing the Organisation of the Cabinet" which was adopted in 1955 the cabinet posts were further increased to twenty-four ministries and two committees (the state planning committee and the state construction committee). A few more specialised ministries for such things as heavy industry, light industry, chemical and construction materials, electricity, marine products, and urban construction were added.

The era of First Five-Year Plan (1957–1961) marked a further consolidation of the administrative apparatus. With the election of the second session of the Supreme People's Assembly on August 17, 1957, a new cabinet was organised. Unlike the Soviet Union, which took decisive steps to decentralise its economic administration, North Korea continued a course of centralisation by amalgamating various specialised ministries. The functional approach to central control is asserted by a North Korean jurist:

> The decision of the Party and government regarding the establishment of local industry and the reorganisation of the structure and control system of central ministries and bureaus, has been put under way at the proposal of Premier Kim. This decision is another indication of the creative character of state control under the guidance of the Party.[17]

By integrating the specialised ministries into two councils of heavy industry and light industry the number of ministries was reduced to twelve. Thus, the ministries of Electricity, the Coal industry and the

[16] Pak Chang-ok, Deputy Premier and Chairman of the State Planning Committee; Kim Il, Deputy Premier and Minister of Agriculture; Choe Chang-ik, Deputy Premier and Minister of Finance; Chong Il-yong, Deputy Premier and Minister of Heavy Industry; Pak Ui-wan, Deputy Premier and Minister of Light Industry.

[17] "Reorganisation of the Structure and the Control System of Central Ministries and Bureaus," *Minju Sabop* (*Democratic Judicial Administration*), September 1959, p. 3.

Chemical industry have been unified into the Ministry of Power and Chemical Industries; the ministry of the Fishing industry has been merged into the Ministry of Light Industry; functions of the Purchasing and Food Administration Ministry have been transferred to the Commerce Ministry; and the ministries of Labour, Local Administration, Urban Construction, and Justice have been abolished. These measures were taken to expand the functions of the local administration giving them some incentive for efficiency and effective control.

The process of simplifying the government structure has greatly affected the legal administration in North Korea. Despite the Soviet legal reform of December 1958, North Korea pursued the integration of the judicial and executive branches in the administration of justice. The functions of control over the judicial administration, including state arbitration by the Ministry of Justice, was transferred to the Supreme Court with the abolition of the Ministry of Justice. According to the words of one North Korean jurist,

> This unification is highly significant in the development of our judicial system. It will strengthen not only the Central Government's supervision and control over trials and court proceedings, but also enable local courts to realise, through their trials, Party policies and platform with flexibility and accuracy thereby contributing greatly to the further consolidation of the legal order and the acceleration of Socialist construction in our country.[18]

The same author asserted that North Korean jurists had already envisaged the eventual integration of courts and law enforcement agencies in March 1950, but that it had taken several years to execute it. By Cabinet Decision No. 52 which was adopted on March 13, 1950, "Decision Concerning the Abolition of the Justice Department at the Provincial People's Assembly and the Revision of the Table of Organisation of the Courts at All Levels," the Justice Department at the Provincial People's Assembly had already been abolished and its functions transferred to the Provincial Courts. But the Ministry of Justice and the Supreme Court maintained independent authority over the law enforcement agencies and the court, and this in turn created confusion and problems. For example, when a lower court conducted a trial in accordance with directives from the Ministry of Justice, the Supreme Court, if its opinion differed from that of the Ministry, could reject or modify the judgment pronounced by the lower court. In such a case, the lower court would be bewildered; some lower courts would follow the opinion of the Ministry of Justice while others would follow that of the Supreme

[18] Yi Pong-gol, "Necessity and Significance of Unifying Courts and Law Enforcement Agencies," *Minju Sabop* (*Democratic Judicial Administration*), October 1959, p. 4.

Court. It has also been argued that a more efficient implementation of Party policies and programmes through court proceedings necessitated the unification of the courts and law enforcement agencies. "All our judicial organs must act in unison in accordance with the unified will in the course of implementing Party policies." [19] In failing to copy Soviet trends toward decentralisation, North Korea might have been pursuing a Chinese line.

The events following the death of Stalin and de-Stalinisation in the Soviet Union created repercussions in the political and legal professions of North Korea.[20] Debates about establishing the rule of law and socialist legality raged not only in the Party's Central Committee but also in the legal profession. Those "anti-Party factionalists" who had linked themselves with the views of revisionism and had opposed the Party line were subsequently purged from the Party. Announcing the complete elimination of the "anti-Party group" from the Party in March 1958 the Party intensified its Party-line propaganda and ideological indoctrination. The Conference for Prosecutors and Judicial Administrators was called in April 1958, the so-called "anti-Party factionalists" were condemned and the Party's judicial policy was defined by the Premier and Minister of Justice.

According to Premier Kim's condemnation, the "anti-Party factionalists" accepted the international doctrine of revisionism and advocated that "law should be applied equally to everyone" and "human rights should be upheld." [21] These people had also interpreted the people's democratic dictatorship as not equivalent to the dictatorship of the proletariat. They had been misled because North Korea was still pursuing the united front policy. Premier Kim explained, however, that the North Korean system of government is in fact the dictatorship of the proletariat because North Korea was in the stage of socialist construction. He pointed out that the North Korean jurists must uphold the law as a weapon to safeguard the socialist system and the dictatorship of the proletariat already established in North Korea.

After the conference, "a vigorous class struggle" was reported to have been carried on within judicial institutions in order to implement the Party's judicial policy. Those jurists who advocated the "humanist approach to law" and the "democratic system of law" were purged from both the legal profession and the Party, and all opposition to the

19 *Ibid.*

20 Development of legal thinking since the death of Stalin: see John N. Hazard and Issac Shapiro, *The Soviet Legal System: Post Stalin Documentation and Historical Commentary* (New York: Parker School of Foreign and Comparative Law, Columbia University, 1962).

21 Kim Il-song, *op. cit.*, p. 439.

Party and government policy was silenced. On the achievement of the post-conference period a North Korean jurist wrote:

> Great achievements were recorded in the liquidation of the injurious effects of the Rightist defeatism advocated by anti-Party counter-revolutionary factionalists. That group attempted during the post-war period, and especially in 1956, to ignore the Party's leadership over judicial institutions. Under the pretext of the independence of judges and Socialist legality they wanted to paralyse the functioning of the dictatorship of the proletariat often assisted by the judiciary organs." [22]

Anyone who has observed the North Korean political scene for the past decade or so will have concluded that North Korea has persistently pursued the centralisation of its administration, yet it has not found a suitable solution to its problems. After the most recent election to the third Supreme People's Assembly on October 8, 1962, the cabinet was reorganised. This recent cabinet reorganisation indicates that more posts have been created in the central administration while the local administrative organs still remain as they were at the time of the last reorganisation of 1958. This may be an indication of a desire to create more posts at the top for the participation of the younger managerial class and technicians who have become a source of concern to the North Korean leaders. In addition to the posts of the Premier, the First Deputy Premier, seven deputy premiers, and thirteen previous cabinet posts, ten fresh cabinet posts have been created. These cabinet posts cover social safety, metallurgical and chemical industry, electric and coal industry, machine industry, marine products, urban industrial construction, agricultural construction, grain purchase and administration, labour, and urban construction. There are also five cabinet committees; state planning, state construction, state science and technology, light industry, and agriculture.

Out of these complex administrative organs North Korea is attempting to work out some kind of administrative theory that can be applicable to a newly emerging industrial society which had once been a backward agrarian society. The transition from the agriculture-oriented society to a semi-industrial society has created new social strata: managerial technicians, administrative bureaucrats in the Party and governmental apparatus, and an intelligentsia educated in the Soviet Union, Communist China or Eastern Europe. The success and failure of the North Korean administration will largely depend on how it controls and adjusts to these new diversified views and how effectively it utilises them in the administrative system.

[22] Yi Pong-gol, *op. cit.*, p. 6.

*The North Korean People's Army and the Party**

By KIWON CHUNG

WHEN a revolutionary movement seizes power, a Communist one no less than others, it faces the extra-revolutionary task of establishing a loyal and efficient military organisation to consolidate its conquests. In order to ensure unchallenged loyalty, the leaders of the revolution must, first of all, fill the army with their supporters. In order to secure an efficient phalanx, they are at the same time compelled to professionalise their fighting force. However, in the midst of a profound socio-political upheaval, these two objectives are not easily fused into one. The North Korean People's Army (NKPA), however, was in a unique position for its strengthening processes from its foundation in 1945. First of all, the NKPA did not need to fight against well-equipped Japanese forces. Secondly, it did not face such complex problems as the dispersal of enemy officer cadres, the securing of enemy loyalty and sympathy, a Civil War and its aftermath, all of which had caused considerable worries to the Communists in the Soviet Union and China. When absolute loyalty is doubtful, officers' professional qualifications are a dubious asset. The Party can never relax its leadership for the sake of a more professional army.

BACKGROUND: CREATION AND DEVELOPMENT

The formative period of the Democratic People's Republic of Korea (DPRK)—from August 1945 to September 1948—was from the outset directed toward the creation of a Stalinist system through the three stages of revolution or tactics described by Seton-Watson: genuine coalition, bogus coalition and the monolithic block.[1] These terms, coined out of the experience of central and eastern Europe, acquired a unique pattern in the case of North Korea. Of great significance were the absence of indigenous political forces, the after effects of Japanese military colonialism, the availability in large numbers of trained Koreans long resident in the Soviet Union.[2] There was thus a political vacuum in

* I thank Dr. Glen W. Baxter, Director of Harvard-Yenching Institute, who kindly rendered me financial aid to make a trip to the Library of Congress for the preparation of this paper.

1 Hugh Seton-Watson, *From Lenin to Khrushchev: The History of World Communism*, 6th ed. (New York: Frederick A. Praeger, 1960), pp. 248–249.

2 Already in the First World War, the Russian Koreans proved themselves loyal subjects of the Czars. Four thousand of them served in the Russian Army, including

which, during its military occupation, the Soviet Union had sufficient opportunity to establish a satellite to its own taste. Already in the first stage of genuine collaboration, the Soviet Union was well aware that without an effective power instrument made up of "native Koreans," total control could not be exercised.

The divergent response to Soviet control was to a great extent conditioned by the arrival of repatriates from Yenan in north China in December 1945. As a result, the monopoly of "people's democracy" held by the Russians and their man Kim Il-song was threatened. In Yenan in July 1942, these revolutionaries had organised politically as the "Korean Independence League" and militarily as the "Korean Volunteer Corps." Such central figures as Kim Tu-bong, Ch'oe Ch'ang-ik, Pak Il-u and Mu Chong (artillery commander in the Eighth Route Army under P'eng Teh-huai) had gained control of a large portion of political and military personnel in the formative period. Mu Chong held the same position of artillery commander in the Peace Preservation Corps (Poandae), the forerunner of the People's Army, and Pak Il-u was in charge of the Ministry of the Interior which, most important of all, controlled the Political Defence Bureau equivalent to MGB in the Soviet Union.

After the stationing of the XXVth Soviet Red Occupation Army in Korea under General I. M. Chistiakov, Kim Il-song's partisan detachment, consisting of no more that fifty men, filtered into the country. These were the remnants of partisan fighters who had been in south-eastern Manchuria, particularly in the Chien-tao region of Kirin Province, until they were forced to retreat to Siberia by the Japanese extermination campaign of 1940-41. Before or in 1942, Kim's new company, composed of Koreans living mainly in Siberia, Khazakstan and Uzbekistan, had participated in the encircling operation on Stalingrad in January 1943. For this, Kim had been honoured with the "Stalin Medal" and the rank of major in the Red Army.[3] Kim Ch'aek, the Commander in Chief of the Front Army during the Korean War, An Kil, the first Chief of the General Staff of NKPA, Nam Il, Chief of Staff in the Rear Army and senior delegate to the Korean truce meeting, all held the rank of either first lieutenant or captain in the Soviet Army.[4]

one hundred and fifty as officers. After Russians and Ukrainians, the third largest ethnic group in the Soviet Far Eastern Republic was Korean numbering 300,000. See Walter Kolarz, *The Peoples of the Soviet Far East* (New York: Frederick A. Praeger, 1954), pp. 32–35.

[3] Tsuboe Senji, *Hokusen no kaiho junen* (*Ten Years of Liberated North Korea*) (Tokyo: Nikkan Todotsushinsha, 1956), pp. 24–26.

[4] *Ibid.* pp. 170–172. Most of the names appearing in this article refer to Kasumigaseki-kai (ed.), *Gendai Chosen Jimmei Jiten* (*A Biographical Dictionary of Modern Korea*) (Tokyo: Ajiakyoke, Gaimusho, 1960).

The consolidation of political power in the hands of Kim's faction and the expansion of the Workers' Party in 1945–47 was accompanied by the growth of the Peace Preservation Corps (PPC). By mid-summer 1946, police training, including that of the Border Constabulary and the Railroad Guards, was already well developed under each local people's committee as well as in various training schools. In particular, the PPC training centre under the Supreme Commander, Deputy-Marshal Ch'oe Yong-kon, now the titular head of the state and originally a partisan leader in north Manchuria, was chiefly responsible for the establishment of a number of special training schools in Pyongyang, Shinuiju, Kech'on, Ranam and Wonsan. There was a coastguard school in Chinnampo and railroad guard schools in other areas. The total force of 20,000 men was well equipped partly with surrendered Japanese weapons and partly with Soviet-made arms.[5]

Under a rapid but clandestine programme, at least 10,000 men, the cream of the youths recruited by selective conscription, were sent to Siberia mainly for military and technical training in Khabarovsk and the Chita Far East Military Academy. Most of them stayed for about three years and returned between 1948 and 1949 to be appointed to the new tanks, aircraft and communications corps of the "peasant but heroic army of the working class," which was expanded to 60,000 men in early 1948. At the first graduation of the Combined-Arms Command School on October 26, 1947, Kim Il-song, then chairman of the North Korean People's Committee, made for the first time a semi-official remark on the creation of a strong army:

> Under conditions in which there exist aggressive forces (Syngman Rhee's forces under the direction of the American imperialists) whose aim is to oppose our fatherland and the people, our government and Workers' Party are confronted with the necessity of founding their armed forces, the People's Army, for building and consolidating the state. . . .[6]

It was not until February 8, 1948, however, that the NKPA was officially activated as a regular army "for the DPRK," but not yet "for the Party." In the fourth session of the People's Assembly on February 6–7, 1948, the draft of the constitution was confirmed as it was proposed by the preparatory committee which had been organised in the previous session in 1947. According to the constitution (Art. 100), "The Korean People's Army is formed for the defence of the DPRK. The mission of the KPA is to safeguard the sovereignty of the

[5] Edwin W. Pauley, *Report on Japanese Assets in Soviet-Occupied Korea to the President of the United States, June 1946* (unclassified on November 8, 1949), p. 119.
[6] V. A. Matsulenko, *Koreyskaya Narodnaya Armiya* (The Korean People's Army) (Moscow: Voennoe Izd-vo, 1959), p. 17.

fatherland and freedom of the people." Thus, at the military parade on February 8, 1948, in Pyongyang, Kim Il-song declared that:

> The Korean people, for the first time in their history, had created armed forces genuinely of the people and capable of defending their democratic achievements . . . [and stressed] the tasks of strengthening military discipline, educating the soldiers in bravery and heroism, and mastering Soviet military science and the valuable combat experience of the Soviet armed forces.[7]

Kim had also asserted that the characteristic of the People's Army was that unlike that oppressive tool, the "capitalist army," it was armed with Marxism-Leninism in general and, in particular, with the inspiration of Stalin's works.[8]

The organisational and personnel components were, as pointed out briefly: (1) Kim's partisan contingent; (2) about 3,000 Korean returnees from Russia led by Ho Ka-ui and An-kil; (3) the Korean Volunteer Corps led by Mu Chong and Pak Il-u; (4) several thousand independent partisan fighters from both Manchuria and north China led by Pang Ho-san, Kim Kang and Kim Ho.[9] Thus, from the very inception, were sown the seeds of fractionalism that bore such bitter fruit in the 1956–58 period of the great purge in the army, as we shall see later.

Ch'oe Yong-kon was appointed to be the first Minister of National Defence; Kim Il, the second man in the country today, Commander of Cultural Affairs (political commissar); An Kil, Chief of the General Staff, under whom were the navy and air force headed by Han Il-mu and Kim Won-mu, respectively. Needless to say, most of the senior personnel were recruited from Kim Il-song's followers and the returnees from Russia, but some Yenan returnees also held substantial posts.

At this juncture, one may ask: Why was the People's Army set up before the appearance of the DPRK on September 8, 1948? Part of the answer undoubtedly lies in the complex factors of political change. One of these factors was the complete failure of a Joint U.S.-Soviet Commission to resolve the question of unification and withdrawal of both the Soviet and U.S. occupation armies. Another factor was the whole relationship of North Korea to the Soviet and the Chinese Communists, and in particular, the relationship with Lin Piao's field army during the crucial war in Manchuria. During the abortive Joint U.S.-Soviet Commission meeting, the overt creation of a People's Army would have belied the notion of peaceful unification and would have provoked unnecessary repercussions from without. But when, early in

[7] *Ibid.* pp. 17–18.

[8] *Kim Il-song Sonjip* (*Selected Works of Kim Il-song*) 2nd ed. (Pyongyang: Choson Rodongdang Ch'ulpansa, 1954), IV, pp. 348–351, 355–356.

[9] Kim Ch'ang-sun, *Pukhan Sip-o Nyonsa* (*Fifteen Years of North Korean History*) (Seoul: Chimungak 1961), pp. 61–65.

1947, Lin Piao's field army was forced into retreat by a Nationalist offensive, probably Kim and possibly the Russians became increasingly alarmed lest the Yenan factions should feel encouraged by the proximity of Chinese Communist forces, and called for the rapid creation of military forces.

Despite this precaution, sometime in 1947, Li Li-san, then in charge of labour affairs in China, visited North Korea and concluded a mutual assistance agreement, providing Manchurian food stuffs in return for North Korean military aid. The agreement resulted in the entry of some 100,000 youths chosen mainly from among the two million Korean minority in Manchuria and partly from North Korea. Another secret agreement was concluded in December 1947, in which Communist China recognised the "North Korea People's Committee" as the legitimate government of Korea. Subsequently, in early March of 1948 a Soviet-Chinese-North Korean Joint Military Council (*Haptong kunsa hyoepuihoe*) established its headquarters in Pyongyang "to co-ordinate certain military activities of the three Communist Parties."[10] (It was this Council which was to co-ordinate the work of both the Soviet military advisers and the Chinese People's Volunteers (CPV) during the Korean War.[11]) It is not difficult in this context to understand that during the Korean War, Peking was repaying a debt to Pyongyang. Nor was it strange when Mao Tse-tung said at the time the CPV crossed the Yalu River: "The bright five-starred national flag of the People's Republic of China was also dyed with the blood of the Korean revolutionaries."[12] It was thus hardly a coincidence that the first foreign delegation which rushed into Pyongyang on the fifth anniversary of the "liberation" (August 15, 1950) with a gift of 100,000 blankets and enormous quantities of medicine was a Communist Chinese delegation under Li Li-san, then Minister of Labour.[13]

No sooner had Lin Piao's army taken over Manchuria in 1948 than North Korea undertook an intensified programme for the reinforcement and militarisation of the NKPA. This was completed after a one-year programme under the supervision of the Soviet advisory group which was set up on the withdrawal of the Soviet Army. These Soviet advisers are said to have been specially instructed "to possess the knowledge of the Korean language and Korean customs." It is also said that "several Soviet general officers and a number of field grade officers were attached

10 Robert B. Rigg, *Red China's Fighting Hordes* (Harrisburg, Penn.: Military Service Publishing Co., 1951), pp. 278–279. Also, see Kim Sam-kyu, *Konnichi no Chosen* (*Korea Today*) (Tokyo: Kawade Shobo, 1956), pp. 34–35.

11 *Ajia Keizai Junpo* (*Ten-Day Report of Asia Economics*), No. 94, December 1950, pp. 1–8.

12 *History of the Just War for the Liberation of the Fatherland of the Korean People* (Pyongyang: Foreign Languages Publishing House, 1961), p. 138.

13 Tsuboe Senji, *op. cit.*, p. 84.

to the National Defence Ministry " as well as to the military academies and the naval training schools where they were acting as instructors. The allocation of advisers was thought to have been as many as 150 per division, but the number was reduced to twenty per division and one per company after the fulfilment of the one-year programme.[14]

Military conscription before 1949, was on the basis of semi-volunteers at the rate of 20,000 men per year from the age group eighteen to twenty-two. Prepared quotas were sent down by way of the provincial and county people's committees and of the leading social organisations such as the Democratic Youth League. Where the quotas were not met, direct coercion was resorted to; police force was used to bring in conscripts. But the system of conscription was not, even as late as 1961, universal; according to a recent defector's information, the sons of high Party and government officials continued to be treated differently.[15] It seems also to be true that urban workers are less liable for army service than are peasants. The placement of conscripts is made on the basis of family composition, education and individual aptitude for the necessary requirements, except that unless the conscripts are considered truly " red " they are placed away from the 38th Parallel lest they should defect to South Korea.

Before the Korean War, manpower was rapidly increased by about 20,000–22,000 returnees from Manchuria (who served under Lin Piao's Korean Communist Volunteer Forces). They formed the NKPA 5th, 6th and 7th divisions, later known as the " dare to die corps " in the Korean War.[16] In addition, there were more returnees thereafter so that Manchurian veterans made up approximately " one third of the NKPA " in early 1950. Prior to the Korean War, a total estimate of military forces reported twenty-four divisions: six spearhead divisions, two armoured divisions, eight infantry divisions, eight militia divisions (or local army, Chipanggun), consisting in all of 200,000 to 300,000 men. Estimated weapons were: about 500 T-34 tanks and armoured vehicles, about 200 YAK-9 fighter and reconnaissance planes and about thirty mosquito vessels—all of Soviet make.[17]

[14] U.S. Department of State, *North Korea: A Case Study in the Techniques of Takeover* (Washington: Publication 7118, Far Eastern Series, 103, 1961), p. 114.

[15] Kim Yon-hoe, *Ot'on Kwisunja ui sugi* (*A Defector's Diary*) (Seoul: Newoe Munchae Yonkuso, 1962), p. 69.

[16] Robert B. Rigg, *op. cit.*, p. 279. At about the same time, over 5,000 Soviet-Koreans who served in the Soviet Red Army poured into North Korea. See *Sovieto Nanken 1954* (*Soviet Year-Book 1954*) (Tokyo: Nikkan Todotsushin-sha 1954), p. 801. Some technical accounts are in, Roy E. Appleman, *United States Army in the Korean War: South to the Nakton, North to the Yalu* (June-November 1950) (Washington: Department of the Army, 1961), p. 9.

[17] For a different account, see Roy E. Appleman, *op. cit.*, pp. 8–12. *Sovieto Nenkan 1954*, *op. cit.*, p. 801. Kim Ch'ang-sun, *op. cit.*, p. 266.

The Korean War

The early People's Army was, however, a poor organisation from a professional point of view. Military discipline was virtually non-existent. A glaring deficiency was the absence of well-trained personnel to fill the higher command and staff posts. The predominantly peasant composition of the army was bound to cause the leadership concern. While the Party through cultural command pursued its educational programme with unremitting effort, at the same time it had to concern itself with disloyal elements from the village being introduced into the army and the prevalence of peasant habits. Furthermore, the centuries-old basic social structure did not melt away in the short period of the "people's democracy." The Confucian tradition of consanguinity continued to interfere with the demand for a new loyalty—"soldiers armed with Marxist-Leninist-Stalinist ideology." Although the peasant soldier was exalted as a hero of the working class, the demands of the three isms were too much for the "idiotic and lazy" class, as Marx called them.

To counteract widespread rural opposition to conscription, hostages were held during the war to exert pressure on the head of the family. Also, lack of technical training and administrative management, combined with the practice of embezzlement, was a serious hazard to the army. Kim warned at the meeting of internal security and political cadres that "there still remain many vestiges of Japanese officialdom, bureaucratic pretensions and corruption." The fact that "you all get dressed up in military uniform," Kim continued, "does not mean that you have to act like the Japanese police or army . . . think of the fact that in the past the Korean people had neither their own government, party, nor army." [18]

The very next day after the outbreak of the Korean War on June 25, 1950, a Seven-Man Military Committee was organised to co-ordinate all operational, administrative and ordinance activities relating to the army and was vested with "authority to mobilise the entire forces of the country." [19] The chairmanship was held by Kim Il-song, premier and chairman of the Party; Hong Myong-hui, deputy-premier; Pak Hon-yong, deputy-premier and foreign minister; Kim Ch'aek, deputy-premier and minister of industry; Ch'oe Yong-kon, Minister of National Defence; Pak Il-u, Minister of the Interior and the only Yenan returnee; and, Chong Chun-t'aek, National Planning Commissioner.[20] On July 1, the Presidium of the Supreme People's Assembly (SPA) had effected a

[18] *Kim Il-song Sonjip*, *op. cit.*, pp. 88–95.
[19] Tsuboe Senji, *op. cit.*, pp. 80–81. Also see *History of the Just War for the Liberation of the Fatherland . . .*, *op. cit.*, p. 39 (hereafter *History of JFLW*).
[20] Tsuboe Senji, *op. cit.*, p. 81.

total mobilisation in the age group of seventeen to twenty-five. Within a few weeks, " volunteers from all organisations, notably from Komsomol and Kim Il-song University and others, reached 849,000." At the same time various movements such as " Front Brigade," " Youth Work Team," " Front Shock Workers," " Doing two or three shares More," " Double Production for the Front," and other groups aiming at increased production, were launched in the rear front.[21] On July 4, Kim Il-song was appointed the Supreme Commander in Chief of the NKPA, to whom the Front Army under General Commander Kim Ch'aek, the Chief of the General Staff Kang Kon, and the Rear Army under Chief of Staff Nam Il, and Kim Yol, chairman of the organisational department (*orgburo*) of the Party Central Committee were directly responsible.

The qualifications of a Supreme Commander have not been laid down by the constitution or any other statutory provisions. However, the appointment to it is within the jurisdiction of the Presidium of the SPA. But the functions of the Cabinet include " to direct the formation of the NKPA, to appoint and remove high ranking officers of the NKPA " (Art. 55). In theory, the Cabinet is " subordinate to the SPA in its work and is responsible to the Presidium of the SPA when it is not in session " (Art. 60).[22] Most important of all, this Committee had in theory controlled the Joint Military Council which meant that the CPV was under the Supreme Commander, Kim Il-song. There is ample evidence that all messages as well as military orders were signed by Kim but not countersigned by General P'eng Teh-huai, the Commander of the CPV.[23] The function of the Joint Military Council seems to have ceased after the armistice in July 1953 when both Marshal Kim Il-song and General P'eng were awarded the title of " Hero of the DPRK." [24]

It is also interesting to note that the Medal of the Fighter for the Liberation of Korea and the Medal for Combat Service were introduced by the Presidium in 1948 and 1949, respectively, before the official ranks of officers were clearly distinguished in December 1952. Soldiers called each other " comrade." According to the decree, the People's Army officers were classified into fourteen ranks: marshal, deputy-marshal, senior general, general, lieutenant-general, major-general, senior colonel, colonel, lieutenant-colonel, major, senior captain, captain,

[21] *History of JFLW*, *op. cit.*, pp. 75–76.

[22] The Constitution written in Japanese is in *Chosen Voran* (*A Survey of Korea*) (Tokyo: Kaigai Jijo Josasho, 1960), pp. 221–229 (translations are mine).

[23] *Kim Il-song Sonjip*, 2nd ed. (Pyongyang: Choson Rodongdang Ch'ulpansa, 1954), III. This volume covers the period from June 26, 1950, to November 30, 1951, and contains 34 speeches, messages and orders relating to the army.

[24] V. A. Matsulenko, *op. cit.*, p. 124. On February 8, 1953, Kim was appointed Marshal by the Presidium of the Supreme People's Assembly, p. 124.

first lieutenant and second lieutenant.[25] Medals were to be given to all soldiers regardless of rank.

As the initial stage of the war proved favourable to the NKPA, " mass heroism " and " private bravery " were recognised and rewarded by the Soldier's Order of Valour (first and second class). The Supreme Commander's order No. 7, dated July 5, 1950, had established that a title could be conferred on squadrons. For example, the 3rd and 4th infantry divisions and the 105th tank brigade, who had rushed into the city of Seoul, were awarded the title of " Seoul " and the 105th tank brigade was promoted to tank division. These divisions fought bravely at the crucial battle of the Nakton River and were honoured with the title " Guard Division." Again, in memory of the death of Kim Ch'aek, the 4th division was permitted to bear his name and hence was called " Kim Ch'aek-Seoul-Guard the 4th Division." [26] The bearers of titles were given superior weapons. The highest honour, the medal of " Hero of the DPRK," entitles the hero's family to special privileges.

There is in fact an interesting comparison between Kim's nationalistic appeal in the Korean War and Stalin's Pan-Slavism during the Second World War. Calling the war " The Liberation of the Fatherland " and " Great Patriotic War " in his broadcast to the entire army, Kim spoke of Korea's historical heroes. " Aggressors," he said, " are out to exterminate the Korean people and oppress and colonise a nation of such great generals as Olji Mun-dok, Kang Kam-Ch'an and Admiral Yi Sun-sin." [27] On the fifth anniversary of liberation on August 15, 1950, Kim exhorted the soldiers to go into the war remembering " the manly image of our great ancestors' glorious achievement and militant tradition." He went on to say:

> The national liberation struggle, which the Korean people are waging for the freedom and independence of their fatherland against the U.S. imperialists who attempt to enslave them, does not arise from a transient or temporary cause but from the fundamental national aspiration of the Korean people *who do not wish to become slaves*

[25] *Sovieto Nenkan 1954*, *op. cit.*, p. 801. It was classified into 13 ranks and in 1958 made into 14 ranks. The added rank was that of senior general, see Kim Yon-hoe, *op. cit.*, pp. 80–81.

[26] *Kim Il-song Sonjip*, Vol. 3, pp. 15–16, 231–233. For a simple account of the situation of the army in 1952, see Yinozaki Kiyota, " Hokusengun no ichi genkyu " (" A Study of the North Korean Army ") *Continental Problems*, III, No. 11 (November 1954), p. 26.

[27] *Kim Il-song Sonjip*, III, pp. 30–31. Olji Mun-dok was one of the greatest generals in Korean history, who in A.D. 612 exterminated Sui Yang-ti's invading army at Pyongyang. Kang Kam-ch'an was also an heroic general who in A.D. 1018 achieved a great victory over Khitan's invasion near Seoul. Admiral Yi Sun-sin, who defeated Toyotomi Hideyoshi's invasion (1592–98), is considered to be the creator of the Korean navy. His triumph over the Japanese naval force in the southern sea is still discussed and praised by all Koreans. See *Chosen Jinmei Jisho* (*Who's Who in Korea*) (Seoul: Government-General of Korea, 1937), pp. 1, 1168–1169, 635–637, respectively.

> *again to foreign imperialists after experiencing long enslavement under Japanese imperialism*. . . . For this very reason, the Korean people will be victorious (italics supplied).[28]

In the war years, Korea as the fatherland completely overshadowed the stereotyped phrases of " Great Liberator Stalin " and " Fatherland of Socialism." In short, Kim found it expedient to neglect the themes of people's democracy and international proletarianism and to stress nationalism and patriotism as politically and socially unifying objectives. By military standards the whole army appears to have fought bravely, but to what extent the quality of the fighting was a consequence of " ideological conviction " is difficult to assess. In fact, it is doubtful whether indoctrination had very much effect on the rank-and-file soldiers.

As the continuation of the war tarnished the hope of victory, a new trend began to evolve. The paramount goal of the preceding era in the history of the NKPA had been the transformation of the army into a dependable Party instrument. At the third Plenum of the Party Central Committee on December 21, 1959, Kim analysed the causes of the great weaknesses in the People's Army in his report on " The Present Situation and Immediate Tasks." " What is, and was, wrong with us?" Kim demanded. He listed them as: (1) the insufficient preparation of the reserve army against an unexpected threat by the U.S.; (2) the inferior quality of defensive and administrative lines; (3) the incredible lack of military discipline; (4) the incomplete extermination of the enemy which allowed it a breathing spell to reorganise; (5) the inadequacy of both night and guerrilla warfare, particularly of surprise attacks on staff headquarters; (6) infiltration of " poisonous elements " in the rear front resulting in extremely poor supply co-ordination and, most important of all, (7) total lack of political training and revolutionary heroism. " What can we do to ensure victory? ", Kim asked. In order to instil the soldiers with firm ideas as to what they were fighting for and why they had to fight, " the Party organisation and a disciplined body of well-versed Party members should be infused into the People's Army." [29] As a result, " at the personal suggestion of Supreme Commander Kim Il-song " this Plenum adopted a decision to " Introduce Party Organisations and to Institute Political Organs in the People's Army " [30] in order to strengthen ideological-political work among the officers and men.

Prior to this, political-cultural work was in the hands of cultural-commandants directly responsible to the Cultural Commander, Kim Il,

[28] *History of JFLW*, *op. cit*., p. 113.
[29] *Kim Il-song Sonjip*, Vol. 3, pp. 124–173.
[30] *Ibid*. pp. 142–143.

of the Defence Ministry, but not to the Party Central Committee. There were no Workers' Party cells in the army, except the one social organisation, Komsomol, which was allowed to inject itself into the company units. The cultural commandant's position in the corps-regimental level was part of a dual system of command which was bound to be fraught with possibilities of friction. First, all orders were to be countersigned by the military commander and by the cultural commandant. Secondly, it was an extremely difficult job to balance the competing demands of professional *esprit de corps* and the cultural commandant's directives. The result has been shown in the purge of 1950–51 at the division command level, according to Kim's own words, " due to the absence of political work and individual heroism." Such military figures as Kim Han-chung, Ch'oe Kwang, Kim Yol and, most of all, Mu Chong, then Commander of the Second Corps, were all demoted. Strangely enough Kim Il was also stripped of his position as cultural commander.[31]

Meanwhile, the new system seems in principle to have provided for a " one-man command " in the army. The command would retain full control of all combat training and economic administrative work, Party work and the political and moral guidance of the unit, while the general direction of Party organisation and the evaluation of training and morale would remain under the control of the political commander of the General Political Bureau (GPB), which would be directly responsible not to the National Defence Ministry, but to the propaganda department of the Party Central Committee. At the same time, the Party infused a complex but highly centralised system of Party organs which penetrated every aspect of army life. Party organs and cells were established in all military units above battalion level, and the Komsomol section of the GPB was in charge of platoon units and below.

Komsomol leaders are subject to the political commandant of the higher units. To be a young commander in a proper unit (usually also secretary of Komsomol in the unit) it is necessary to be a Party member or to be a candidate for Party membership. To be a regular member, it takes one and a half years after the approval of the political commandant at a higher level.

During the Korean War, the Komsomol continued its unremitting efforts to establish its position and to recruit new members into the army. At the Third Party Congress in April 1956, General Kim Kwang-hyop, then Chief of Staff of the army and now Minister of National Defence (since 1957), reported that " more than 76 per cent. of the

[31] *Ibid.* p. 139.

soldiers and 45 per cent. of the officers were Party-Komsomol members." [32]

The function of political commandants varies greatly with their position in the hierarchy and the job to which they are assigned. Regardless of unit level, however, the responsibilities concentrate on supervising the training and promotion of the soldiers, ensuring their positive devotion to the Party, the preparation of political programmes and materials for use in classes, and supplying pamphlets and newspapers, pictorial exhibitions and films. Promotion for the soldier is almost completely dependent on the recommendation of the political commandants whom the rank-and-file soldiers fear more than the professional military commanders.[33] Also, political commandants conduct the political education of the higher ranks under their charge, in addition to reporting every few days on the state of morale. Thus, Kim Ch'ang-pong and Ho Pong-hak, Chief of Staff and Director of the GPB respectively, said in 1961 at a lecture to division commanders, that " you can report directly to your higher officers whatever happens in your division. However, we have to report even trivial things directly to Premier Kim Il-song." [34]

On the whole, the " one-man management " system has considerably strengthened the Party-army relationship. In practice, it is still subject to considerable limitations and allows no room for flexibility. It is tightly restrained by the secret organs of the Political Defence Bureau (PDB) of the Internal Ministry in the army. The role of the PDB is not only characterised by the integrated system of its hierarchy, but also by its unique authority in the army. It may well be described as punitive as its duties are to root out disaffection and disloyalty in the army. Like the MGB in the Soviet model, the PDB has its own troops, navy and air force, including border garrisons and railroad guards. They all wear the same uniform and ranks as the army and are therefore indistinguishable. The PDB had at full strength about 5,000 agents supported by some 12,000 regular police, who had played a great role in the war. It is said that about 100 PDB agents are to be found to a division.[35]

POST-WAR PERIOD: REORGANISATION

As soon as the armistice agreement became effective in July 1953, the régime took a number of stringent measures for rehabilitation, reorganisation and rearmament, as well as making Three-Year (1954–56) and Five-Year Economic Plans (1957–61).

[32] *Third Congress of the Workers' Party of Korea: Documents and Materials* (Pyongyang: Foreign Languages Publishing House, n.d.), p. 179. Also, see *History of JFLW*, *op. cit.*, p. 319.

[33] Kim Yon-hoe, *op. cit.*, p. 106.

[34] *Ibid.* p. 77.

[35] U.S. Department of State, *op. cit.*, p. 39.

It is important to note that an increasing emphasis was placed on the psychological and technical preparation of the people for war and on the unity of the army and the people. The régime established the "National Liberation War Medal" to be conferred not only upon the army and CPV, but also upon state institutions, public organisations, military units and provincial and rural organs of the people's committee. Taking the opportunity at the 8th anniversary of the liberation on August 15, 1953, more than 746,000 civilians were awarded the medal in addition to 480 soldiers and thirteen units of the army. An army-people rally was organised which featured street dancing and lasted three days.[36] The people were also encouraged to visit the "War of Liberation Museums" being built in every province and city where war trophies and commemorative oil paintings were displayed. Some typical titles of paintings are as follows: "Battle on Height 1,121," "Mother of Pak Chae-won, Peasant and Martyr," "Sons and Daughters of the DPRK." Films circulating throughout the country bore titles such as: "Young Partisans," "Never Again Will We Live That Way." "The CPV and the People." The content of one of the films is worth quoting:

> Jo Ok Hi, the first woman hero of the Republic, was a Party member. When the Eunpa Mountain Partisan Detachment was organised by the underground Party organisation in Byuksung County to resist the enemy which had made its way into the northern part, she was one of the first who joined the detachment. She was in charge of supply services for the staff . . . finally she fell into the enemy's hands. They subjected her to every kind of brutal torture in an attempt to wring out of her secrets about the partisan detachment. They pulled out all her finger nails. But the enemy always got the same answers: "You fools! No one gets secrets from a Workers' Party member!" The blood-thirsty U.S. cannibals . . . raged. They gouged out her eyeballs, burned her with a red hot iron and cut off her breasts. . . . At last . . . facing the firing squad . . . she told the enemy: "You may kill me here today, but there is our People's Army to revenge my death. . . ."[37]

At the same time, the Party measures for the training and strengthening of officer cadres were of special importance. All troops were merged into the cadre army. The objective was for every soldier to possess "leadership capability" in the event of a unit being dispersed in time of war. In accordance with this, a soldier's schedule requires that he has to attend six hours political education per week. Topics and curricula include both current international and domestic events, the history of the Worker's Party, the history of Kim Il-song's anti-Japanese partisan struggle, the meaning of Socialist patriotism and the

[36] *Third Congress of the Workers' Party . . ., op. cit.*, p. 179. Also, V. A. Matsulenko, *op. cit.*, pp. 105–110.
[37] *History of JFLW, op. cit.*, pp. 133–134.

danger of foreign espionage, and so on. As for informal political education: division and garrison clubs have collections of material illustrating life in other Socialist countries and translations of Soviet publications.

In 1955, the Kim Il-song Military Academy was set up in addition to the existing Kang Kon (who was killed in the war) Combined Arms School, the Kim Ch'aek Military-Political Institute, and the Special Aviation, Navy, Artillery, Tank, Infantry and Medical Schools.[38] Great attention is given to the advanced training of senior command personnel, and their political study is conducted in a special course under the military academy.

Organised grand manoeuvres have been intensified on the inter-divisional, inter-regimental and inter-battalion levels—scheduled once a week in a company, every two months in a battalion, three months in a regiment, six months in a divison and once a year in the armed forces.[39]

The territorial militia (*Chokwidae*) is also an important military development. It is composed of workers, peasants, labourers, the intelligentsia, entertainers, writers and other elements. According to P'eng Chen, a Politburo member of the Chinese Communist Party, who witnessed a militia parade in Pyongyang in May 1962, each regiment consists of twelve squadrons, composed of fourteen rows in each squadron, eighteen men in each row; hence a regiment includes 3,024 men and women. It also has its own medical corps. The militia is armed with automatic rifles and other equipment including armoured vehicles, all of North Korean manufacture. The regiments are led by discharged soldiers presently employed in factories, agricultural co-operatives and schools.[40]

The economic role of the army in many activities in recent years is a noteworthy phenomenon. Following the example of workers' economic competitions such as the "model worker competition," "brigade competition," and the "winged-horse title," the army has applied the same ideas to companies and instituted the "exemplary company movement" and the "red flag company effort." By 1959, the army had adopted a plan for supporting itself. It could either produce its own foodstuffs, by cultivating the land allotted, or by earning some money through irrigation and other massive projects, with the approval of the national planning commission, the ministries of national defence and of agriculture.

[38] V. A. Matsulenko, *op. cit.*, pp. 108–109.
[39] Kim Yon-hoe, *op. cit.*, pp. 78–79.
[40] *Nodong Shinmun*, June 3, 1962.

In 1956, the campaign for disarmament to reduce the size of troops to 80,000 men was launched at the same time as the appeal for south-north unification. Gradual demobilisation was started and the discharged veterans were to be rehabilitated in previously appointed areas where labour forces were most needed. At the same time the national defence budget was cut down from 75,245,000 yen (100%) in 1953 to 56,504,000 yen (75.1%) in 1956, 53,832,000 yen (71.5%) in 1957 and 63,563,000 yen (84.5%) in 1958. In proportion to the total state budgetary expenditure, the percentages were as follows: 15.2 in 1953, 5.9 in 1956, 5.3 in 1957, and 4.8 in 1958.[41] The disarmament was, from the economic point of view, meant to be fitted into the first Five-Year Economic Plan. The need for a greater labour force must have been the principal impelling factor behind the move to disarm. This reasoning is also supported and confirmed in a speech of General Kim Kwang-hyop at the Third Party Congress in 1956:

> Should the enemy provoke another aggressive war against our country, opposing its peaceful unification which is the long-cherished desire of the Korean people, our People's Army is determined to respond to the call of the Party wherever and whenever it may come and to give still greater annihilating blows to the enemy to the last drop of its blood. . . . We will keep a careful watch over the enemy, and further strengthen the fighting preparedness and fighting efficiency of our units, and increase the quality of military and political training. . . .[42]

Although no direct evidence is available, some scanty but suggestive sources indicate that a three and a half year active military law was adopted in the new Regulations for Services of Officers and Soldiers of 1956. Some of the main provisions of the new law are: (1) Military service is of two kinds: active and reserve. Non-commissioned officers and rank-and-file privates serve for a term of three and a half years for the infantry and border troops, and four years for the air force and navy. (2) All male citizens who have reached the age of seventeen to twenty-two have this duty to perform. The period of recruitment is generally in March and August.[43] Before 1956, the service period was seven years. In order to give a leeway, annual leaves were instituted in 1960. Until then, leaves were limited to the group leave for specified recreation at weekends. Probably, the main purpose was aimed at preventing military secrets from leaking out during leaves, or the psychological discontent experienced at facing the poor life in the family.

[41] *Choson Chungang Nyongam* (*North Korean Central Yearbook 1959*), as translated in JPRS (Washington: U.S. Joint Publications Research Service, 2691, May 21, 1960), pp. 187–193.

[42] *Third Congress of the Workers' Party . . ., op. cit.*, p. 184.

[43] Kim Yon-hoe, *op. cit.*, pp. 69–70.

According to 1958 figures, the most recent source available, the ground forces consist of eighteen divisions and five brigades; 540,000 men (some sources quote a figure of about 430,000); 3,000–4,000 trench mortars, about 1,800 tank guns (bazooka), forty-six rocket guns and about 600 tanks and armoured cars. The navy is reported to have over 16,000 men and 160 vessels of various kinds. The air force has about 20,000 men consisting of five fighter divisions, one bomber division, one transportation division and one reconnaissance division. The total number of planes is estimated between 850–900, of which between 150 to 200 are MIG–15s and 50–70 I–L type. Of about forty air bases, thirteen bases are for jets.[44]

In the reorganised structure, the former Seven-Man Military Committee was replaced by the National Defence Ministry. The military figures of the People's Army are as follows: [45]

Kim Kwang-hyop: Senior General, Minister of National Defence, Deputy-Premier (ex-Kim Il-song partisan comrade), and a full member of the Presidium of the Party Central Committee.

Ch'oe Hyon: Senior General, Vice-Minister of National Defence (ex-Kim partisan comrade), and a full member of the Presidium of the Party C.C.

Pak Kwang-son: Lieut.-Gen., Vice-Minister of N.D.

Kim T'ae-hyon: Lieut.-Gen., Vice-Minister of N.D.

Kim Pong-ryul: Lieut.-Gen., Vice-Minister of N.D., and a candidate member of the Party C.C.

Kim Ch'ang-pong: Senior General, Chief of the General Staff of the NKPA, and a full member of the Party C.C.

Ho Pong-hak: Senior General, Director of the General Political Bureau of the NKPA, and a full member of the Party C.C.

Ch'oe Kwang: Lieut.-Gen., and Commander of Air Force.

Sok San: Minister of Internal Affairs and a full member of the Party C.C.

Military representation in both the government organ and the Party is higher than in other Socialist countries. It seems that the same standards are also applied to the local people's committees, according to the constitution (Art. 12): "Citizens serving in the People's Army have the right to elect and to be elected to state organs." Nine out of seventy-one of the Party Central Committee were military generals elected at the Third Party Congress in 1956; three out of nine were added to the full membership list of the Presidium—Deputy-Marshal Ch'oe Yong-kon, Senior General Kim Kwang-hyop and General Nam Il. The reconstruction of the membership of the Party Central Committee, which followed

[44] Nakayasu Yosaku, *Kankoku Tokuhon* (*Korean Textbook*) (Tokyo: Jijitsushin-sha, 1960), pp. 158–160. I have also compared with *Sekai Nenkan 1957* (*World Yearbook 1957*) (Tokyo: Kyoto tsushinsha, 1957), p. 125.

[45] *Nodong Shinmun*, June 10, 1962. See *Gendai Chosen Jimmei Jiten* as explained in note 4. The Commander-in-Chief of the navy has not been identified since 1957. Until then, Lieut.-Gen. Han Il-mu was in charge of it.

the Fourth Party Congress in September, 1961, showed a striking difference. The membership was enlarged to seventy-five and four military generals were dropped from the Party Central Committee, and three new generals were elected to full membership; they were, Senior General Kim Ch'ang-pong, the same Ho Pang-hak and Major-General O Chin-u. The two members of the Presidium have not been changed.[46]

It should also be noted that most of the present generation of high-ranking officers are of a different background, being products of the Korean War period. Such is Ryu Kyong-su, the first raider in Seoul city after the outbreak of the war, who rose to the rank of Lieut.-General and became a member of the Party Central Committee in 1956, and was eventually promoted to General in 1958. Also Im Ch'ol, the present commander of the 13th Division, was only a squad leader during the war. It is equally important to note that the Yenan returnee officers, who were a substantial element in the army and who were a cause of great unease to the Kim Il-song clique, are now almost completely exterminated as a consequence of war, which presumably presented an excellent test-ground for loyalty and devotion to the Party.

The consolidation of the People's Army in the hands of Kim's dictatorship has been secured, but not without an organised terror. During 1953–56, the purge gathered momentum in army circles, but its climax was reserved for the remnants of the Yenan returnees. In late 1957, the purge included an ever-widening military circle and resulted in wholesale removals and arrests of high-ranking officials. The list of the purged includes : Mu Chong the commander of the 2nd Corps ; Pang Ho-San the veteran commander of the 6th Corps ; General Kim-Ung then Vice-Minister of National Defence ; Senior General Yi Kwon-mu the Chief of the General Staff; Lieut.-General Ch'oe Chong-hak then Director of the General Political Bureau; Major-General Kim Ul-kyu then (Deputy) Vice-Director of the General Political Bureau ; and many divisional commanders [47] (for the new appointees see above).

While the available information is insufficient to justify any sweeping conclusions, the indictment against the purged embraced the usual combination of treason, diversion and espionage. And, to what extent this purge can be examined in the light of the dynamics of de-Stalinisation in 1956, and of Left-Right wing tensions in the CCP in late 1957, we do not know.

However, we do know that there is a constant battle between Party control and military professionalism in the army because of the

[46] Kim Ch'ang-sun, *op. cit.*, pp. 152–153. See *Nodong Shinmun*, September 12, 1961.
[47] Kim Ch'ang-sun, *op. cit.*, pp. 140–141. Kim did not mention the date of the purge but " Pang was purged." See *Gendai Chosen Jimmei Jiten*. A general account of the purge is given in *Kim Il-song Sonjip*, V (1960), pp. 317–347.

dramatic coup headed by Lieut.-General Chang P'yong-san in early 1958. Chang's coup throws light on the Party-army relationship *vis-à-vis* Kim's monolithic power at its peak. Lieut.-General Chang was, from his youth, trained in the Eighth Route Army in Yenan and, during the Korean armistice meeting, he concurrently held the position of senior delegate and Deputy-Chief of the General Staff under Lieut.-General Nam Il, the chief delegate. He is said to have planned to dethrone Kim Il-song on May Day 1958 " in alliance with a disgruntled internal faction " and with his own 4th Corps stationed in the outskirts of Pyongyang. At dawn on May Day, the *coup d'état* was turned into a counter-coup.[48] Unfortunately, we do not know whether Chang's corps was crushed by the regular army or the internal police army. At any rate, the chain reaction displaced all Yenan returnees. Was this then simple factionalism in the army? Kim's speech on the tenth anniversary of the NKPA gives an answer:

> Some workers in the General Political Bureau do not agree with the fact the People's Army belongs to the Party. . . . There are many faults with Party education in the army . . . [But] we have to practise " one-man-management " under Party control because the People's Army is the army of the Party and controlled only by Party leadership and because it is the armed force for the fulfilment of revolutionary tasks proposed by the Party.[49]

Kim has criticised the diseased existence of " family-ism," " provincialism " and " sectarianism," furthermore:

> There is a tendency towards separatism in the Party and the army which generates " warlordism " day by day. The cardinal problems are lack of iron discipline and self-criticism . . . the Party will fight continually against these phenomena.[50]

The internal convulsions accompanied by an abortive coup are clearly reflected in the new resolution of the Party Central Committee in March 1958. According to this resolution, a primary Party cell is set up even at company and platoon level. For the surveillance of daily life, a bureau for the primary cell composed of three to five members is elected at a cell meeting. The bureau elects a chairman and a secretary. In the regiment, Party membership is held by 30–40 per cent. of the personnel. At the same time the direction of political indoctrination has been completely reshuffled from the previous emphasis on "learning everything from the Soviet Army" to "the glorious revolutionary, patriotic tradition and the priceless experiences of the anti-Japanese partisans led by Marshal Kim Il-song." Since 1959, we find these stereotyped

48 Kim Sam-kyu, " Senri no koma undono haikei " (Background of the Leaping Horse Movement), *Korea Review*, III, No. 24 (September 1959), pp. 4–5.
49 *Kim Il-song Sonjip*, V, pp. 318, 343–346.
50 *Ibid*.

catch-words in every speech by military figures on all occasions. On the fourteenth anniversary of the People's Army in 1962, Kim Ch'ang-pong, Chief of the General Staff, addressed the rally in Pyongyang:

> The Korean People's Army which has inherited the glorious tradition of the anti-Japanese partisans . . . is organised with the revolutionary fighters as its core . . . developed into a mighty and modern army, with a high political character, by mastering military arts. And since its inception, it has been boundlessly faithful to the Party, the fatherland and the people.[51]

An editorial entitled " The Glorious Armed Forces of Our Party and People " in the *Nodong Shinmun*, the organ of the Party Central Committee, on the same occasion read in a rather unusual fashion:

> The People's Army is a unique revolutionary army that is to destroy the old society and to construct the new society in a revolutionary manner. It is to protect the fruit of revolution which is obtained by the struggle of the Party. Advancing along the revolutionary path under the guidance of the Party, the People's Army is only loyal to the order of the Party . . . following the direction of the cadre army as proposed by the Party in the post-war period, the formation of the People's Army has been more firmly organised than ever in its ideology, modern military science and technological weapons.[52]

Whether the motivation of the search for " identity within national tradition " lay in internal political maturity or developing " domesticism " towards Sino-Soviet tensions, is a difficult and perplexing question to evaluate in the scope of this article.

Conclusions

Obviously, the NKPA is in a period of stabilisation and is being consolidated into the poltical apparatus of the Party. The fact that the People's Army is " only loyal to the Party," as Senior General Kim Ch'ang-pong, Chief of the General Staff, stated on the fourteenth anniversary of the NKPA in 1962, ensured the régime unrivalled monolithic power which should not be lightly dismissed. Yet, potential danger lies in the nature of the institution itself: there is resentment of intensive indoctrination, particularly among the rank-and-file soldiers, and the tensions between the amount of authority of the political commanders and the responsibilities of the military professionals could be a source of trouble.

As a recently escaped soldier revealed, the grievances of the soldier are chiefly concerned with harsh discipline, the special status of the officer corps, and the use of break hours and short intervals for rest for

51 *Nodong Shinmun*, February 8, 1962.
52 *Ibid.*

political education. But these complaints present no serious threat to the top inner circle. First, unceasing propaganda will create in the long run its own immunities, if not apathy and inertia. Secondly, in spite of these discontents, most officers' ranks recruited from peasant origin find themselves unconsciously holding the image of an antagonistic outside world and pride in the economic achievements, which may constitute a cementing factor with the Party régime. Finally, the role of the Komsomol in the age group from sixteen to twenty-five cannot be disregarded because of its active participation in every aspect of army life. They have been and are totally sealed off from without so that their emotions and thinking are subject to complete control.

Will there be any chance of Bonapartism? It seems unlikely. Various circumstances constitute an effective system of checks: a firm military alliance with the Soviet Union and Communist China (signed in July 1961), and backing by these two gigantic Powers; the small, easily suppressed population of less than eleven million; more directly, constant surveillance by both political officers and PDB agents inspires fear and mutual suspicion which results in inactivity.

Until 1958, when the Yenan returnees held a substantially higher position in the army, the margin of disaffection and dissension was considerably higher. And they were the only faction that could stand directly opposite to Kim Il-song's clique, which has now taken over the inner core of the army. There may be some Yenan returnees who have survived through a number of purges, but they are insignificant without their leaders. Again, higher military officers are either represented in the Supreme People's Assembly or in local people's committees and are of special élite status. Needless to say, they do not want to risk the vested interest they have acquired in the survival of the régime.

Undoubtedly, relations between the political commanders and the military officers offer a fertile ground for friction. However, this should not be interpreted to mean that the Party leadership stands in any imminent danger of losing its control of the armed forces. Kim's use of the "divide and rule" principle in the appointment of a national defence minister in the Presidium of the Party Central Committee has in a large sense the effect of annulling frictions among most ranks.

As long as the political and police controls in the army remain centred in the hands of a unified Party leadership, it is improbable that the army will emerge as an independent political force. But if the Party apparatus itself weakens as a result of a bitter inner-Party struggle or by large-scale war, only then may the army have the opportunity to be an independent force. And it seems most unlikely.

North Korean Educational System: 1945 to Present

By KEY P. YANG AND CHANG-BOH CHEE

AN examination of the educational objectives of North Korea and the system which implements these objectives reveals the true image of a country only dimly perceived since it disappeared behind the Bamboo Curtain after its liberation from the Japanese in 1945.

Most Western observers tend to equate North Korean objectives with those of other Communist countries; this is especially true in regard to Communist China. The present educational system of North Korea, however, supports the assumption that the country is in the throes of redefining its own cultural heritage along strong nationalistic lines as a means of paving the way toward Communism under the banner of proletarian internationalism led by the Soviet Union.

The most distinguishing feature of the present North Korean educational system is its rebirth from the bitter ashes of Japanese colonialism and, more recently, from the destruction of the Korean War. Unlike the educational programmes of most Communist countries, the North Korean system is not the product of the revision and remodelling of a traditionally accepted nationalistic form of education.

Even before the Japanese occupation with its stringent measures designed to obliterate Korean culture, a self-imposed submission to Chinese culture existed in Korea. A circumstance which antedates the Yi dynasty (1392–1910) has been Korea's lack of both opportunity and initiative to promote an expressly indigenous educational curriculum tailored to the needs of her own particular society.

Against this historical background, the principles of education in North Korea can be characterised by three primary objectives: (1) the socialistic reorientation of the younger generation and the adult population in the direction of the "Communist man"; (2) the revival of nationalistic patriotism; (3) the promotion of the educational concept of integrating theory and practice or "learning and labour." Under these broader objectives there emerge two concrete and immediate goals which focus on providing "at least one specialised skill for every person," through universal and compulsory technical education; and on elevating the educational standards of the entire able-bodied population to that of junior high school graduates.

The progress of these ambitious plans can be evaluated through a review of the seventeen years of the present educational system; which can be divided into three stages: (1) the pre-Korean War period, 1945–50; (2) the Korean War period, 1950–53; and finally, (3) the post-Korean War period from 1953 to the present. Each period is characterised by its own distinct objectives, practices and spheres of influence.

1. Pre-Korean War Period: 1945–50

In the early years of the liberation from Japanese domination, Korean education appeared destined to wear the imprint of still another foreign power. Because North Korea was liberated by the Soviet Union and fostered by it as a *de facto* government, a strongly pro-Soviet faction developed in the North Korean government. They successfully insinuated Russian cultural norms into Korean school programmes under the slogan of "Learn from the Soviet Union."

Pictures of Russian heroes were installed in the Korean schools. Mayakovsky and Pushkin looked down from the walls of Korean classrooms on Korean children. Intellectuals preferred Russian terms to Korean terms; even in the compilation of school textbooks to replace the Japanese books, information was derived from Soviet literary sources rather than from Korean literature. There must have been genuine concern behind the question asked by Kim-Il-song in 1955: "How can we teach our children to have national pride." [1]

The immediate objective of the North Korean régime during this early period of social reconstruction (1945–50) was to transform through re-education and reorientation a backward and previously subjugated society into a highly regimented and energetic society. All vestiges of Japanese culture had to be purged from the social order and from the educational programme. The first steps towards realising this objective were taken in 1949 with the revision of textbooks by replacing the centuries-old use of Chinese characters and Japanese language with the previously banned Hangul, or Korean phonetic alphabet.[2] The second objective of this early régime in its efforts to reconstruct society was to institute a compulsory system of education to influence the total population.

This monolithic system envisaged putting all the existing systems into a public co-educational system of free public schools. Japanese schools, which had been used by the Japanese living in Korea, schools

[1] *Kim Il-song Sonjip (Selected works of Kim Il-song)* (Pyongyang: Choson Nodong-dang Ch'ulp'ansa, 1960), IV, p. 330.

[2] Despite the efforts of the South Korean government this change-over to a Korean script has not yet been accomplished in South Korea.

endowed by religious organisations, private schools and girls' schools[3] were all to be consolidated into one government-controlled educational system. This plan for universal, free education under a compulsory system was interrupted in 1950 by the Korean War.

The third objective in this period was the literacy campaign for adults. At the end of 1944, 2·3 million Koreans were illiterate. Within a few years after the Second World War, North Korea successfully eradicated illiteracy. This became a good propaganda weapon in asserting the superiority of socialism over capitalism. During the Japanese administration, only 35 per cent. of school-age children were able to go to school, and only 18 per cent. of those graduated from elementary school went on to high school.

During this pre-Korean War period Soviet educational advisors were assigned to teachers' colleges to train teaching cadres. It was revealed that there were thirty such advisors in Korea in 1949.[4] By the end of 1949, 620 college students had been sent to the Soviet Union for higher education.[5]

2. The Korean War Period: 1950–53

The Korean War which began on June 25, 1950, resulted in the destruction of 90 per cent. of all cultural and educational facilities. During this period 850,000 students, about one-half the total number of students in North Korea, were mobilised for war. Schools were organised mostly underground or deep in the mountains. Teachers and students remaining behind were also mobilised to do espionage work or operate as guerrillas, propagandists or agitators.

This was the period when patriotism and a nationalistic fervour swept through the rank and file of the North Korean population. A sense of fatherland gained new force in a dramatic manner; new heroes and heroines were created, and "*Tangsong*" ("party spirit," equivalent to the Russian *partiinost*) loyalty to the party, was emphasised. This new nationalistic tendency was evidently reflected in education. Kim Il-song, the North Korean Premier and Chairman of the Korean Workers' Party since 1948, added national dignity and a sense of national identity to the objectives of his political movement. This new objective was considered of maximum urgency because of the task of reconstruction and because of the presence of Chinese troops in North Korea. This objective of instilling a sense of national identity in the Korean people began a new educational trend which differed from the pre-war directives of modelling the Korean educational system on the Soviet pattern.

[3] Girls' schools exist now as technical schools.
[4] *Kim Il-song Sonjip, op. cit.*, 1954 ed., II, p. 535.
[5] *Ibid.* pp. 233, 399.

Not until 1953 did schools again open in even a semi-complete state. New educational needs and the rehabilitation problems of orphans, wounded war veterans and war widows resulted in the establishment of special schools offering training in accounting, handicrafts and trades. A considerable number of orphans were sent to other Communist countries. Rumania alone took care of 1,500 orphans who were not returned to Korea until the five-year economic planning period from 1957 to 1961.[6] These orphans trained in foreign languages, plus the students in Korea who study languages in their eleven-year language training schools (from the first grade of elementary school) will provide North Korea with a sizeable reservoir of language experts. In addition to these foreign educated children, nearly 80,000 Koreans by the end of 1962 will have been repatriated from Japan since 1959. Of this number, 40 per cent. are school-age youths. This bilingual element in the present Korean society is an educational accomplishment and advantage worth noting.

Besides these, college students and technical trainees were sent to the Soviet Union and other Communist countries for study. Kim Il-song disclosed that 5,000 were sent to other countries during this period for technical training alone, with the anticipation of their service during the three-year economic plan (1954–56). It was revealed later that they were all returned to North Korea during the years 1954–56.[7]

Other than the newly emerging sense of national unity arising from the war period and the establishment of the Academy of Sciences in 1952,[8] little concrete progress was made in the educational system during this time.

3. Post-Korean War Period: 1953–

After the material devastation of the Korean War the task of reconstruction became a matter of rebuilding the social structure and the physical condition of the country. An educational doctrine that expounds the dignity of labour and the necessity of the individual student fusing his own goals with those of society was particularly useful to the political régime whose responsibilty it was to rebuild the economic life of the country in the shortest possible time.

The Marxist emphasis on the dignity of physical labour, has been used to convince the students that the time-honoured scorn of the

[6] *Kim Il-song Sonjip, op. cit.*, 1954 ed., IV, p. 167.

[7] Yi, Nag-on, " Inmin kyoyuk saop e taehan Konghwaguk chongbu ui sich'aek " (" The government policy on popular education "), *Inmin*, No. 8, August 1956, p. 69.

[8] The Academy of Sciences was established in 1952, but its influence and its development were impeded by the war years; therefore, it will be discussed briefly as an institution of the Post-Korean War period. Its activities are so important and complex that to do it justice a special study of the North Korean Academy of Sciences should be made.

classical Confucian scholars for any common physical labour is in conflict with the goals and ideals that characterise the "New Socialist Man." The student is taught that his own self-realisation will be accomplished through promoting the achievements of his society; he must identify with the goals of society by fusing his personal objectives with those of the group.

Persuasion through governmental discipline in cases where discussion groups and self-criticism sessions have failed seems to have extinguished most of the bourgeois spirit of individualism that flickered in the early days of the liberation. Reactionary problems seldom exist, especially on the student level, because these students are a new generation whose minds have been moulded by the pervasive idea of the ultimate dignity of the labourer and the superiority of the proletariat.

The school system incorporates a theory-practice concept of education in which the theories of the classroom are translated into active participation in government-directed labour units designed to consolidate the student's learning and also to assist the government in its effort to industrialise the country. This segment of Korean society probably would not have developed to such an intense degree if it had been offered only the abstract concepts of international Communism. The educational system's life-oriented, purposeful theories of learning are supported basically by the Marxist ideology of the dignity of labour as the origin of all value and wealth, it is true; but these educational theories are enhanced and become particularly potent motivational devices when an emotional appeal to national pride and national identity becomes a stimulating force within a society.

Credit for the resurrection of an indigenous educational system must be given to Kim Il-song. During the Korean War a pro-Chinese faction in the government contended on points of theory with the pro-Russian faction. The victorious faction would ultimately have shaped the future of North Korean education in the pattern of the educational system of the foreign country to which the prevailing faction offered its allegiance. Kim Il-song silenced the contending groups, decrying "those who returned from the Soviet Union wanted to follow what the Soviet Union did, and those who returned from China insisted in following China. They argue that they are correct. Is it not nonsense?" [9] and then concluded, "Is the time not ripe for us to have our own way?" [10]

In 1955 Kim Il-song delivered his now famous speech positing his thesis of "*Chuch'e*" (national individuality) to a conference of Agit-prop cadres. According to its author, Kim, *Chuch'e* is defined as a theme for the socialisation of Korea along distinctly Korean lines:

[9] *Kim Il-song Sonjip, op. cit.*, 1960 ed., IV, p. 335.
[10] *Ibid.* p. 336.

> We must make our régime suit the characteristics of our own country. . . . The first requisite for *Chuch'e* is the realisation that we are carrying on a strictly Korean revolution. This Korean revolution is the *Chuch'e* and the core of our Party. . . . Therefore, what we are studying of Soviet Communist Party history, what we are studying of Chinese revolutionary history, and what we are studying of the general theories of Marxism and Leninism must all be directed towards the proper Korean revolution.[11]

The goal of Kim's revolution is to inculcate a sense of pride and national individuality or *Chuch'e* within the Korean people. Kim's revolution is moving against the great odds of centuries of educational philosophy that traditionally minimised the Korean heritage and culture while either glorifying Chinese culture or imitating Japanese culture. This fact together with the Korean people's own concept of their country either as a backward, hermit kingdom, or as China's vassal state make Kim's task a formidable one.

Kim's major objective is to erase from the minds of the Korean people their concept of themselves as the isolated poverty-stricken, hermit people of the Yi dynasty, and their more recent memories of themselves as an enslaved people who helplessly submitted to the colonial yoke of Japanese imperialism. To erase from the minds of the Koreans this concept of themselves as a subjugated, inferior people, Kim has instituted a pervasive and systematic study of Korea's historical and cultural heritage.[12] In most courses in the Korean schools the teachers endeavour to instill the students with a sense of pride in their nation's contributions to the cultural progress of the East. Research movements in North Korea indicate that Koreans have a distinct culture of their own, which can be identified among the cultural patterns of the Far East. It is especially apparent in the subject-matter of the archaeological research work conducted by the North Korean Academy of Sciences.

In order to give the impression that Communist ideas in North Korea originate from Kim Il-song and also to create a " Kim-ism " in the mind of the average North Korean, Kim is depicted as the " benevolent father." The study of Kim Il-song's teachings, including the history of his partisan movement, is placed before the teachings of dialectical materialism, and even prior to Marxism and Leninism.

[11] Kim Il-song's clear nationalism in the quoted statement should not lead one to think of him as a kind of Tito. In the past seven years he has expressly stated that national Communism as founded by Tito's Yugoslavia was unacceptable. See, for instance, the handbook on North Korea entitled *Democratic People's Republic of Korea* (?1958), p. 294. See also *Kim Il-song Sonjip, op. cit.*, 1960 ed., Vol. 4, p. 326.

[12] Kim instructed Korean women to dress in Korea's traditional costumes, not in the increasingly popular Western styles introduced by contact with Russia. *Kim Il-song Sonjip, op. cit.*, 1960 ed., IV, p. 336.

Every organised institution prominently displays either a bust of Kim Il-song or a picture of him. Each institution has a facility or a special room dedicated to the study of Kim Il-song. These rooms are generally known as "history rooms." Every citizen of North Korea is required to read the works of Kim Il-song. He is portrayed as the origin of the highest knowledge and his words are revered as the epitome of learning.[13]

Kim Il-song in a speech to his people stressed the necessity for enormous efforts to overcome the backwardness of their country and thereby provide the people with a future they can look to with pride as well as a distant historical past on which to base their national identity. "While others go one step forward, we must move ten steps forward." [14] Kim symbolises the new Korean spirit that looks to future accomplishments.

The desire to make Korea distinct among the nations of the Communist bloc rather than a follower is strikingly apparent in Kim's educational goals, many of which have already been realised. Education since 1954 has followed in the path of the country's economic plans; the Three-Year Plan, 1954–56; the Five-Year Plan, 1957–61; and the Seven-Year Plan, 1961–67. The educational objectives outlined for each period by the government have apparently been carried out in the most expeditious manner largely because of the interest and insistent urging of Kim Il-song himself. Kim's writings and speeches are replete with rhetorical questions such as: ". . . in order to live better than others, is it not necessary for us to dash to catch up, instead of running? Running is insufficient." [15] Kim's programmes to socialise his country have been implemented by putting into effect a series of short-term projects.

A. *The Three-Year Plan, 1954–56*

The Three-Year Plan which was announced soon after the armistice, July 27, 1953, was designed to prepare the basis of heavy industry. This emphasis on industrialising the country was reflected in the immediate objectives of the educational system. The educational plan for 1954–56 had four basic aims: (1) to rehabilitate all educational facilities to the status of 1949 (pre-Korean War) and, if possible, to exceed that goal; (2) to increase the registration of students at the various school levels;

13 In addition to these forms of adoration, monuments, museums, and memorials have been erected in his honour and to preserve his personal belongings. Even a spot where he stayed overnight is preserved as sacred. These are all open to the public as "living classrooms," as they are called. Furthermore, all North Korean publications take their cue from the words of Kim Il-song.

14 *Kim Il-song Sonjip, op. cit.*, 1960 ed., VI, p. 112.

15 *Kim Il-song Sonjip, op. cit.*, 1960 ed., V, p. 561.

(3) to offer compulsory four-year elementary education by 1956; (4) to prepare ways and means to expand secondary school facilities to accommodate future graduates from the newly established system of compulsory elementary education.

In order to achieve these goals, an all-out effort was vigorously pursued. On construction sites it was common to see even girl students putting caps over their dangling hair and pushing wheelbarrows side by side with the boys. As a result, by the end of 1955, school facilities were rehabilitated quantitatively to the level of 1949. Two million students were attending five thousand schools. It was at this time that elementary schools were established at the ratio of two schools in every *ri*, the lowest political division, with an average population ranging from 2,000 to 2,500 split among 400 to 450 households. Compulsory four-year elementary education was finally enforced by the autumn of 1956.

The economic plan gave priority to heavy industry, especially to the machine industry, and vocational education was stressed to meet the needs of technical manpower. During this period a new type of technical high school and college with a course lasting two or three years was established. There were 66,072 students in 127 such colleges, which were not high quality technical institutes but offered what by Western standards would be apprenticeships. These colleges are to be abolished after 1962 due to the reorganisation of the educational system which began in 1960. New types of universities such as construction universities and economics universities for the training of engineers and managers were also established. There were 22,458 students in nineteen universities by the end of 1956.

The rapid rehabilitation of educational facilities and the swift turnout of teachers resulted in mediocrity in the educational field. It was stated by Kim Il-song at the third Congress of the Korean Workers' Party held in April, 1956 that:

> The basic defect in school education is that teachers' thought and intellectual level are low; the content of education lags in scientific and thought analysis; there is a bureaucratic attitude in school administration; and finally, teachers teach what is considered alien to the political and economic life of our country.[16]

Kim Il-song, in 1956, also pointed out poor organisation of technical institutes. For example, at a training school where workers' children under fifteen years of age were recruited for technical training in agriculture, the students did not know what they were studying and for what purposes because of poor organisation and teaching. Therefore,

[16] *Kim Il-song Sonjip, op. cit.*, 1960 ed., IV, p. 564.

Kim Il-song suggested that the students be sent back home and be allowed to learn the trade of their parents.[17]

Another significant feature during this period was the return home of North Korean students and trainees from abroad. By 1955 those who had been sent abroad during the Korean War period had returned. By August 1955, five hundred students who had finished college or post-graduate work, and six thousand technical trainees had returned.[18] During 1957, another group of 1,263 returned home (of which 1,000 were technical trainees, 150 were university graduates from the Soviet Union and other Communist countries, and 113 were graduates from Communist Chinese universities).[19] Thus a total of 7,763 had returned home by 1957.[20]

B. *Five-Year Plan, 1957–61*

Immediately following on the Three-Year Plan, North Korea launched its First Five-Year Plan under the slogan of preference for heavy industry but with stress on the simultaneous development of light industry and agriculture. Unlike the outgoing Three-Year Plan which aimed at the rehabilitation of the economy to the level of 1949, the Five-Year Plan aimed to construct more industries in order to solve the problems of the people's livelihood, so they would not have to worry about " what to eat, what to wear, and where to live."

Ironically, however, Kim Il-song disclosed an insufficiency of consumer goods in 1959, the year when the Five-Year Plan was supposedly achieved. In order to correct these mistakes, 1960 was designated a " Wanch'unggi " or " buffer period " for the purpose of adjusting past mistakes and improving prefabricated construction, and relaxing the work drive as well as producing more consumer goods.

Although there were failures in this plan, a considerable expansion in industry was accomplished under the slogan of " Ch'ollima " (" one thousand mile leaping horse ") introduced in December 1956.

Again, the educational programmes of the country were adjusted to meet the new demands of a society attempting almost literally to lift itself by its own bootstraps from a quasi-feudal, agricultural society to the status of an industrialised Communist nation.

17 *Ibid.* p. 427.

18 *Choson T'ongsa* (*History of Korea*) (Tokyo: Hagu Sobang, 1958), III, p. 441.

19 *Choson Minbo* (*Korean People's Press*) (Tokyo), July 11, 1957, p. 1.

20 The policy of sending students abroad was designed to train highly specialised technicians who could not be trained in North Korea and was adopted out of necessity; since 1959, this policy of sending students abroad has been drastically cut down except in a few instances of special training.

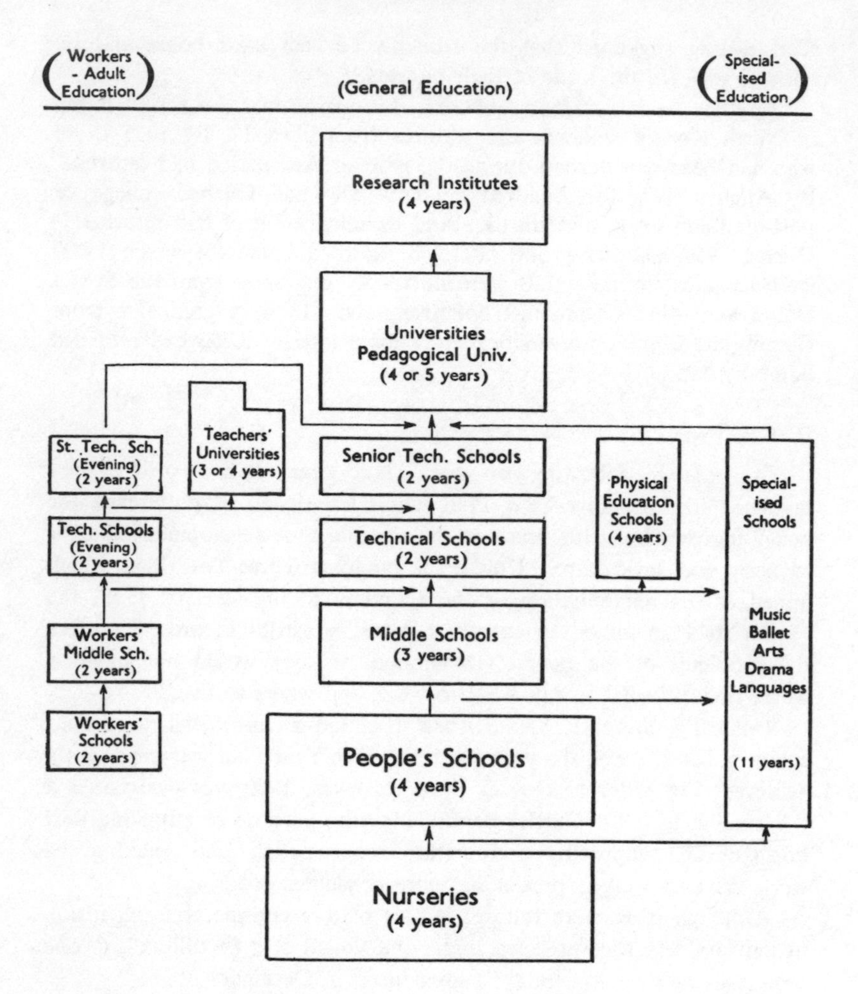

(1) *General educational system.* In the educational sphere, the Five-Year Plan introduced major changes to cope with the technical man-power requirements of expanding industries. The most drastic change in education was the abolition of three-year senior secondary school system and the technical colleges, and their replacement with two years each for both the technical school (previously senior secondary school) and technical senior school systems (previously college level), a unique system which differs from the systems of both Russia and China. This change, among other things, was proclaimed in a Cabinet decision of March 2, 1959, entitled "Reorganisation of the Educational System."

Subsequently, in 1960, the Ministry of Culture and Education was subdivided into three ministries: Culture, Common Education, and Higher Education.

According to this new system, a North Korean child whose merits enabled him to get a university education would have acquired a licence for a profession by the age of twenty-three. Starting at seven years of age, after kindergarten, a student goes to a four-year elementary school, then to a three-year middle school, followed by a two-year technical school and a two-year technical senior school, after which he may attend a four- or five-year college course. (See chart.) If his talent for art is noticed at an early age, he also goes to professional schools for music, dance and sculpture for eleven years or until he is eighteen years old. These professional schools were first established during the 1960–61 school year under the reformed system. Children with an aptitude for languages can also receive such treatment. The eleven-year language-training programme (which includes English) is designed to fill the need for language specialists by 1970.[21] Foreign languages are also taught at Kim Il-song University and Kukche Kwangye Taehak (University of International Relations). Through state examinations, the government issues a licence to those who speak foreign languages.

Another significant feature during this five-year economic planning period was the enforcement of a seven-year compulsory system of free education from 1960. It was the first seven-year programme to be adopted in the Far East; China and Japan have six-year compulsory systems with tuition only partially free. Because students perform their share of productive labour, the tuition-free provision does not really cost the government any money. On the contrary, it is the government which is actually indebted to the students for their service to the state.

Despite this successful education programme, the students looked miserable during this period due to lack of material benefits. It was common to see students shabbily dressed, some of them with unwashed faces and uncut hair. Even the teachers did not shave, the suits they wore were not properly ironed, and often buttons on their coats had fallen off. Some women teachers looked as if they had carried baskets on their heads, because they did not comb their hair.[22]

(2) *Teacher-training education.* Great emphasis was given during this period to training teachers by establishing teachers' colleges with three- and four-year courses, and pedagogical universities with four- and five-year courses. The colleges are aimed at supplying teachers

[21] This system is far more thorough and inclusive than the language programmes of either Russia or China. In Russia foreign languages are not introduced until the fifth grade. In Communist China language study is not undertaken until senior secondary school.

[22] *Kim Il-song Sonjip*, 1960 ed., VI, pp. 15–16.

from nursery school to middle school level (equivalent to the American junior high school). The university is responsible for teachers for technical schools and for the universities. Another institution for training teachers is the recently established teacher-training department set up in every technical university in order to meet the need for the expanding technical high school system. The Pyongyang Pedagogical University, in particular, plays a leading role as the senior institute among teacher-training schools. It has post-graduate courses, research facilities, and a library which is the central national library for educational publications and materials. All the publications and materials relating to the study of education, and textbooks used from nursery schools to the universities, are required by law to be submitted in duplicate to this library for permanent custody on behalf of pedagogical researchers. Ideological and technical preparation is stressed throughout these various systems of teacher-training. The government has placed great emphasis on preparing the teacher ideologically so that he may successfully represent and also convey to the students the ideals of " the New Socialist Man."

(3) *University education.* In 1961 there were 97,000 students in 78 universities in North Korea, of whom 65 per cent. were either technical or engineering students. The population of North Korea in 1961 was 10,789,000.[23] This indicates that the total university student body comprises ninety students per 10,000 population.[24]

Another form of university is the so-called Factory University which was set up in 1960 in major industrial establishments. Its operation is reported successful and more universities of this type will be established. Post-graduate work is also organised in selected universities. This is four-year work with emphasis on research. The first two years are given to classroom lectures, and the final two are for actual participation in laboratories, or research departments of industry. A thesis is also required for graduation. It is not written during the four-year term, however, but upon experience after graduation. There are various research organisations in North Korea headed by the Academy of Sciences. (Research is designed to solve the problems of current programmes; it is not usually pursued for its own sake.) These research organisations are major employers of such post-graduate students.

The pinnacle of the educational hierarchy is the doctoral institution which was established in 1961 in three universities and in the Academy

[23] It was disclosed by Kim Il, the First Deputy Premier, in his speech at the Fourth Congress of the Party on September 16, 1961.

[24] The number of university students per 10,000 population in other countries is as follows: Communist China, 13; Japan, 73; South Korea, 57; the Soviet Union, 107; and the United States, 180. Claude Bissell, " China makes big strides in education," *Washington Post*, September 30, 1962.

of Sciences. The three universities are Kim Il-song University, Kim Ch'aek Polytechnical Institute, and Pyongyang Medical University. Candidates for the doctorate are selected from those whose allegiance to the Party is unquestionable, whose eminence in their fields is recognised, and who have completed two years in practical technical work. So far only a very small number have received the doctoral degree. A planned increase in the number of doctorates during the seven-year economic plan has been reported.

Kim Il-song University is worthy of mention because it is the senior university and the sole university in North Korea which has liberal arts colleges. It is a co-educational university located in the outskirts of Pyongyang overlooking the Taedong River. This is the counterpart of Moscow University and Peking University. Admission is considered the highest honour for North Korean youths. The most competitive and most popular departments are the physics and international relations departments. During the school year 1961–62, there were 12,100 students (5,600 day and 6,500 evening and correspondence students), fifty-four lecture chairs, and 1,000 teachers and staff members. Post-graduate courses are offered in eleven fields including history, philosophy, Korean language and literature, foreign languages and literatures, economics, law, physics, mathematics, chemistry, biology and geography. Besides these facilities, there are thirty-two research rooms in eight research institutes. By 1964 the student body is expected to expand to 20,000 upon the completion of a new twenty-three storey building and a new library.

(4) *Special education and adult education.* Numerous special institutes exist for training various personnel for managerial, political and espionage duties. Some are open, others are secret. The important ones are those institutes under the Cabinet, the ministries, and the Korean Workers' Party for the training of the administrators and officials of Communist universities; there is one Communist university in every province and one in Pyongyang, for the training of Party leaders. (North Korea now contains nine provinces.)

In October, 1957 at the Central Committee Meeting of the Party, Kim Il-song took public cognisance of the necessity for the whole society to move forward technically and ideologically. He pointed out that the goal of the current educational reforms was the creation in the future of a skilled society dedicated to socialist principles, but the country could not afford to concentrate its educational efforts on the young while neglecting the adult population which was, for the present, the very backbone of the Party's success and progress. Subsequently, Kim presented to the Fourth Party Congress in September 1961 a pervasive programme of adult education that stretched its tentacles of influence down to the smallest village unit. Kim promoted his new programme as a " technical and intellectual revolution."

Kim's new directives were aimed squarely at the more recalcitrant minds of the older workers. The present workers were to be elevated intellectually so they would be capable of fulfilling the technical requirements of industry, and they were to be converted to the socialist ideal of accepting the goals of society as one's own personal objectives. The individualism and " reactionary " tendencies of the tradition-oriented workers were to be purged, and workers were to be persuaded to seek their self-realisation through helping society to achieve its goals. This desire to contribute to " the good of the whole " was to be strengthened by the technical training offered under the same educational programme. Under the organ of the Scientific Knowledge Dissemination Federation, educational centres were set up in every political unit: province, district, city, county, village and collective farm. " Democratic Propaganda Class Rooms " were opened in libraries, factories, farms and residential settlements. This new wave of compulsory education raised the amount of education available for the total population to a new level.

Adults are encouraged to attend night schools or participate in correspondence courses to bridge the immediate gap of supplying educated and committed adult workers for the technical jobs that must be filled immediately if North Korea is to continue its " thousand-mile leap forward." The government probably selects correspondence students for scholarships for foreign study to remove the stigma attached to such courses.

A closely co-ordinated effort exists between the general education programme and the adult worker education programme. More than half of the total number of new students entering universities are from the ranks of adult workers. Their records are said to show that students with working experience are academically more successful than younger inexperienced students. This record offers great encouragement to adults and promotes the government's plans to elevate the intellectual and technical abilities of the total populace.

The government's drive to encourage adult labourers to resume their education has both practical and ideological motivations. In a practical sense, the return of adult workers to the classrooms will ultimately lift the educational standards of the country, while demonstrating the socialist principle that learning (theory) and work (practice) are inseparable from the viewpoint of total social development. Ideological considerations are also served through the promotion of the socialist concept that there is no distinction between the intelligentsia and the working class.

C. *The Seven-Year Plan: future perspectives: 1961–67*

The future of North Korea is already conditioned by the Seven-Year Plan (1961–67). Currently, the plan emphasises the development of light industry to produce more consumer goods. From 1964, however, the remaining years of the plan will see a concentration on heavy industry. This economic plan places general emphasis on automation, electrification, and the mechanisation of industry.

In education, the Seven-Year Plan aims to increase technological cadres and there is a new emphasis on turning out scientists. This fact was expressed by Kim Il-song at the Fourth Congress of the Party:

> Our goals must be to open new fields of science, to introduce the latest achievements of science and technology into the national economy and to develop the important domains of the basic sciences. Even research work for introducing atomic energy into production should be carried out under a far-reaching programme and radioactive isotopes and radio-rays should be widely applied in various fields including industry and agriculture.[25]

Upon the completion of the Seven-Year Plan, North Korea expects to surpass Japan in overall productivity, as the Soviet Union and Communist China have set their goals to surpass the United States and Great Britain, respectively.

But over-emphasis on productivity as exemplified by the mobilisation of students resulted in poor performances by the students, even in 1962. It was disclosed that students were pointlessly mobilised, that there was even disorderly conduct by some students, and lack of enthusiasm for their studies.[26]

North Korea's goal in educational affairs for the future is to have the entire population reach the level of technical school graduates of a nine-year compulsory educational system, including two years of technical school—due to begin with the 1964–65 school year. North Korea is even envisaging an eleven-year compulsory educational system, including two years of technical senior school, in the foreseeable future—possibly starting from 1967. In order to achieve these goals, school facilities are expected to be expanded to accommodate one in every four persons. It is also planned to increase the number of higher educational institutions to 227,000 students in 128 universities. The final goal is to obtain 230,000 senior engineers and experts, and 600,000 junior engineers and experts in all fields by 1970. As a result, the number of engineers, technicians and specialists per 1,000 working men and women will be increased from thirty-three in 1960 to 110 in 1970.

[25] *Pinnanun Ch'onghwa Hwihwanghan Chonmang* (*Radiant Aggrandisement and Glorious Future*) (n.p.: 1961), p. 62.
[26] *Inmin Kyoyuk*, No. 1, January 1962, p. 3.

As a result of the continuous economic drive since 1953, North Korea has apparently become the leading example of progress in the Communist camp in the Far East. This claim was made by a Ukrainian lawyer named L. Hudoshnikov who, visiting North Korea in 1960, stated in an article appearing in a Ukrainian-language periodical that: "Among the Socialist nations of Asia, the DPRK was first along the road to establishing Socialism." [27] This view was suggested earlier by Mudo Shuichi, a Japanese observer who favourably compared North Korea's progress with that of Communist China. In 1957, after his stop-over in China and Korea, he said there "was a more immense and compelling air about North Korean construction than about that of the Chinese." [28]

Nowhere are Kim's ultimate plans for North Korea more apparent than in the projected educational programme of his new Seven-Year Plan. He has daringly initiated an inclusive system of free compulsory education that totally surpasses that of either Russia or Red China. The smallness of his country and the unswerving discipline of his régime, plus his past record of accomplishment in the face of great social and economic odds, make his future objectives reasonable possibilities.

Kim's efforts to create a highly organised Communist society imbued with a sense of national identity by exploiting nationalistic tendencies does not necessarily mean segregating North Korea from the Communist bloc; rather, his efforts appear to be focused on making North Korea a showcase in the Communist sphere by adopting the methods, practices and experiences of Red China, the Soviet Union and other Communist bloc nations. The failure or success of this ambitious endeavour depends on the success and extent to which Kim is able to realise his projected plans for the North Korean educational system.

[27] *Radians'ke Prave*, No. 6, 1961, p. 119.
[28] *Minju Choson* (*Democratic Korea*), November 25, 1957, p. 4.

Contributors

Chang-boh Chee was educated in Korea, Japan and the United States. He is Professor of Sociology at Wake Forest College, North Carolina.

Kiwon Chung is studying Communism in Asia at the Graduate School of Harvard University. At present, he is engaged in research on the Fourth Workers' Party Congress of North Korea and the Korean Communist Movement in Manchuria until the rise of Kim Il-song.

Ilpyong J. Kim is a former ROK Army officer, who is currently a Ph.D. candidate in Columbia University's Department of Public Law and Government. He is now preparing a book: *Communism in North Korea: A Documentary History.*

Yoon T. Kuark is currently Instructor of Statistics and Economics, College of Business Administration, University of Denver. He is a Korean War veteran, formerly Air Force Intelligence Officer, Major, Republic of Korea Air Force.

Chong-Sik Lee is an Assistant Professor of Political Science at the University of Pennsylvania, and the author of *The Politics of Korean Nationalism.*

Dong Jun Lee was a writer for *Pravda* in Pyongyang for four years until February 1959. He is the author of *Path to Freedom: Panmunjom* and *Fantasy and Fact: My Observations of Communism,* both in Korean. Since 1959, he has worked as a journalist in Seoul and has written both for the *Seoul Shinmun* and the *Kyonghyang Shinmun.* He has also taught Russian at the Korean Foreign Languages College. He spent the academic year 1962–63 at Princeton University as a Parvin Fellow.

Glenn D. Paige is Assistant Professor of politics at Princeton University and a contributor to the forthcoming symposia on *Communism in Asia,* edited by A. Doak Barnett, and *Communism and Political Revolution,* edited by Cyril E. Black and Thomas Perry Thornton. During 1959–61, he served as research adviser at the Graduate School of Public Administration, Seoul National University.

Robert A. Scalapino is Professor of Political Science and Chairman of the Department at the University of California at Berkeley. His publications include *Democracy and the Party Movement in Pre-War Japan, Parties and Politics in Contemporary Japan,* with Junnosuke Masumi, and numerous articles, including "Origins of the Korean Communist Movement" with Chong-Sik Lee in the *Journal of Asian Studies,* November, 1960, and February, 1961.

Key P. Yang was educated in Korea, Japan and the United States. He is Specialist on Korea in the Oriental Section at the Library of Congress, Washington, D.C.